Moodle Administration Essentials

Learn how to set up, maintain, and support your Moodle site efficiently

Gavin Henrick

Karen Holland

BIRMINGHAM - MUMBAI

Moodle Administration Essentials

First published: July 2015

Production reference: 1170715

Published by Packt Publishing Ltd.
Livery Place
35 Livery Street
Birmingham B3 2PB, UK.

ISBN 978-1-78439-547-6

www.packtpub.com

Credits

Authors
Gavin Henrick
Karen Holland

Reviewers
David Le Blanc
Alexander Angel Corrochano
Sherman Keene
Donald Schwartz
Shashikant Vaishnav

Commissioning Editor
Dipika Gaonkar

Acquisition Editor
Sonali Vernekar

Content Development Editor
Manasi Pandire

Technical Editor
Rupali R. Shrawane

Copy Editor
Charlotte Carneiro

Project Coordinator
Suzanne Coutinho

Proofreader
Safis Editing

Indexer
Rekha Nair

Production Coordinator
Aparna Bhagat

Cover Work
Aparna Bhagat

About the Authors

Gavin Henrick has worked with Moodle in business, learning, and development since 2007. Initially, he worked with Moodle partners in Ireland and Canada, USA, UK, where he gained valuable experience, and in 2011, he started his own consulting firm—Learning Technology Services.

Through the new company, Gavin currently works on supporting organizations with e-learning projects, including Moodle rollouts, hosting and support tenders, Moodle upgrade strategies and processes, and training and best practice workshops.

He is a regular speaker at a number of Moodlemoots and conferences and has organized the UK and Ireland Moodlemoot since 2012.

Gavin recently published the book *Moodle Add-ons* with Michael de Raadt, then the development manager at Moodle HQ. The book provides advice to evaluate add-ons and also helps you identify some great add-ons that will enrich specific aspects of your platform.

He also co-authored the book *Moodle 2.0 for Business Beginner's Guide* with Jason Cole and Jeanne Cole. The book included the key areas that businesses would address in Moodle deployments and included case studies of different implementations.

Gavin has published a number of white papers on Moodle 2 Repositories and Moodle 2 Themes.

Many thanks to Karen for collaborating on this book. It has been a great experience working together on the book.

I would like to thank my family and friends, who have been very supportive of this book and our business.

I would also like to thank the Moodle community for their energy and ongoing development and support of Moodle.

Karen Holland has worked in the programming and technology industry for over 12 years using a range of technologies and languages, including C++, Bash, PHP, CSS, jQuery, XML, SOAP, Git, Symphony, and a number of databases. She has worked as a senior software developer for Learning Technology Services (LTS) for the last 18 months, focusing on the development and implementation of Moodle projects. She has designed and developed plugins and integrations for Moodle and has worked on documenting processes and procedures for use by LTS clients as learning materials.

Karen holds a master's in computer science (NL) from University College Dublin. She also holds a post graduate diploma in multimedia and web authoring and a Joint Education Board (JEB) IT Trainer diploma.

Karen recently presented a Pecha Kucha on Moodle Administration Tips at the UK/Ireland Moodlemoot in Dublin. She also enjoys singing with the Culwick Choral Society and is an avid tennis and rugby fan!

I would like to thank Packt for this amazing opportunity of working on my first book. I would like to thank the Moodle community for their enthusiasm and generosity. I would also like to thank my inspirational sister, Jane, who is a dedicated and innovative teacher, and my parents for emphasizing the importance of education and life-long learning. Lastly, I would like to thank my wonderful partner and co-author, Gavin, for his help, support, and advice while writing this book.

About the Reviewers

David Le Blanc has BA, BEd, and MEd degrees. He is an experienced online guide, Moodle expert, and e-learning practitioner. He has been working on computer-based learning since the mid '80s and in secondary education for the past 26 years. Currently, David works with local school districts and colleges to design online learning and support educators in delivering courses in the Moodle learning environment. Among David's projects is `http://edtechopen.com/`, a collaborative professional development site, which offers free online courses for educators around the world.

He previously participated as a reviewer on two other Packt publications—*Moodle Gradebook – Second Edition* and *Instant Moodle Quiz Module How-to.*

Alexander Angel Corrochano is computer science engineer with more than 10 years of experience in e-learning. As a frontend and backend programmer, especially focused on Moodle, he has developed several plugins, modifications, themes, and implantations of this learning platform. In conjunction with his technical career, Alexander has developed many technical online courses, which have used the full potential of Moodle.

He is also the author of *Novedades para la docencia en Moodle 2.0*, which is available at `http://www.lulu.com/product/ebook/novedades-para-la-docencia-en-moodle-20/16053567`.

I want to thank my wife for her understanding when I have been unable to give her enough time due to work commitments. I would especially like to thank Dani for making each day of my life really interesting.

Sherman Keene was born in New York City, NY, to William (an actor) and Helen (a writer). He grew up in New York City; Miami, FL; Long Island; Hollywood, CA. He has also lived in Montecito, CA (near Santa Barbara); Torrance, CA; Sedona, AZ; Salt Lake City; and Tucson, Arizona.

He played rhythm guitar with Ike and Tina Turner and was a bassist/vocalist with Spirit.

As a recording engineer, his best-known clients were Linda Ronstadt, Ike and Tina, The Turtles, Alice Cooper, The Byrds, and Frank Zappa, for whom he recorded 200 Motels (the movie, album, and single), Live at the Filmore East, Just Another Band From LA, Overnight Sensation, and Apostrophe.

Sherman has written two college textbooks on sound engineering and five books on social awareness commentary.

Continuing with his recording work, Sherman has a Cubase Pro 8 home recording studio where he writes, composes, arranges records, and releases songs he writes and also provides music for films and television.

Sherman writes commercial business software, publishes commercial websites, designs and produces graphical advertising e-mails for clients, and designs and operates a sound engineering Moodle in an online university.

You can visit Sherman at `http://www.shermankeene.com/Sherman_Keene/Welcome.html`, `https://shermankeene.com/classroom` and `http://www.ohmladmusic.com/Ohm_Lad_Music/Welcome.html`.

These sites have e-mail forms that can be used to contact him.

Donald Schwartz has been designing, developing, deploying, and managing Moodle since 2003. He is an expert at giving the video e-learning course presentation and delivery over CDNs to large and disparate clusters of Moodle sites. His clients have included medical societies, engineering schools, and a majority of the ENR top 50 for their CAD software training.

Don's other interest, besides fly fishing, is "wearable computing". He leads the Wearables New England Meetup group and has facilitated hackathons, design sprints, and networking focused on wearables for healthcare in Boston and Washington, D.C.

Donald is the principal of VectorSpect, LLC, a New Hampshire USA-based e-learning consultancy. Prior to striking out on his own, Don spent 10 years developing and building the CADLearning website (`http://www.cadlearning.com/`), an e-learning network for engineering and architectural designers.

Shashikant Vaishnav was born and brought up in the desert town of Jodhpur, Rajasthan, India. He's involved with the London-based seedcamp-supported start-up, shoprocket. It's an e-commerce system delivered over the cloud and integrates seamlessly into any application with a single line of code.

He has been involved with Moodle for quite a long time as a student. While an undergrad, he participated in a Google's Summer of Code program and integrated Apache Solr with Moodle. He also participated as a mentor in the Google code in programme for the Sugar Labs organization.

He graduated from Government Engineering College Bikaner, with a bachelor's degree in engineering and technology in computer science in 2013. His academic focus aside, he harbors a deep interest for music and sports.

He loves to blog about his experiences with open source, technology, travel, and life. He reads spiritual books, is into photography, and hacks around with open source projects.

He previously collaborated with Packt Publishing as a technical reviewer on *Git Version Control Cookbook* and *Moodle 3.0 LTS Administration – Third Edition*.

www.PacktPub.com

Support files, eBooks, discount offers, and more

For support files and downloads related to your book, please visit www.PacktPub.com.

Did you know that Packt offers eBook versions of every book published, with PDF and ePub files available? You can upgrade to the eBook version at www.PacktPub.com and as a print book customer, you are entitled to a discount on the eBook copy. Get in touch with us at service@packtpub.com for more details.

At www.PacktPub.com, you can also read a collection of free technical articles, sign up for a range of free newsletters and receive exclusive discounts and offers on Packt books and eBooks.

https://www2.packtpub.com/books/subscription/packtlib

Do you need instant solutions to your IT questions? PacktLib is Packt's online digital book library. Here, you can search, access, and read Packt's entire library of books.

Why subscribe?

- Fully searchable across every book published by Packt
- Copy and paste, print, and bookmark content
- On demand and accessible via a web browser

Free access for Packt account holders

If you have an account with Packt at www.PacktPub.com, you can use this to access PacktLib today and view 9 entirely free books. Simply use your login credentials for immediate access.

Table of Contents

Preface

Moodle is the world's most widely used open source course management system and is used in over 220 countries, with over 53,000 registered sites. It is built by the Moodle project, which is coordinated by Moodle HQ in Perth, Australia, and supported by over 60 Moodle Partners worldwide.

If you want to deploy Moodle yourself without having to learn everything about the platform and just focus on the key steps, then this book is for you.

The book takes a look at the key aspects of a Moodle setup and configuration. It takes you through the whole project process, from the installation and setup of the site, user account setup and configuration, site structure configuration and site design. It then deals with some key concepts, including user role management, custom plugins, and other essential administrative tasks, such as end of year course rollover.

This book is introduction for Moodle administrators and focuses on the most important options on each settings page, rather than dealing with every single possibility.

What this book covers

Chapter 1, Moodle in a Nutshell, deals with a short background of Moodle. We introduce the architectural structure of Moodle and how the different parts work together. We go through the steps of installing Moodle on a Linux server and also how to perform ongoing upgrades.

Chapter 2, Managing User Accounts and Authentication, deals with the essential areas of user account management that every administrator will have to deal with, including adding a user, bulk adding users, and some of the authentication options.

Chapter 3, Managing Categories and Courses, focuses on building out the site structure of the Moodle site, setting up courses, and also organizing them into categories and sub-categories.

Chapter 4, Managing Site Appearance, examines the ways in which you can enhance the appearance of your Moodle site, extending it beyond the default setup using the existing functionality of Moodle and the available themes.

Chapter 5, Role Management, deals with roles and how they relate to enrolling users onto courses. We look at how you can enhance and extend the permissions of the users, by means of managing their role permissions.

Chapter 6, Managing Site Plugins, explores the options available to enhance the functionality of your Moodle site, extending it beyond the default open source coding code and deals with the essential areas of site plugin management that every administrator may have to deal with.

Chapter 7, End of Year Course Rollover, tackles the end of year course rollover management that every administrator will have to deal with. We look at the issues involved in a course rollover, including course backup, restore, and course reset.

Chapter 8, Miscellaneous Admin Tasks, deals with the remaining essential administrative tasks not covered in the preceding chapters that many administrators will have to deal with, including monitoring Moodle usage, performance testing, security, and resilience.

What you need for this book

You will need the following to work with Moodle:

- A text editor
- An up-to-date web browser
- An SSH client
- Access to a Linux server for installation

Who this book is for

If you are an experienced system administrator and know how to manage servers and set up web environments but now want to explore Moodle, this book is perfect for you. You'll get to grips with the basics and quickly learn how to manage Moodle, focusing on essential tasks. Having prior knowledge of virtual learning environments will be beneficial but is not mandatory to make the most of this book.

Conventions

In this book, you will find a number of text styles that distinguish between different kinds of information. Here are some examples of these styles and an explanation of their meaning.

Any command-line input or output is written as follows:

```
> php automated_backups.php from the /moodle/admin/cli
```

New terms and **important words** are shown in bold. Words that you see on the screen, for example, in menus or dialog boxes, appear in the text like this: "Clicking the **Next** button moves you to the next screen."

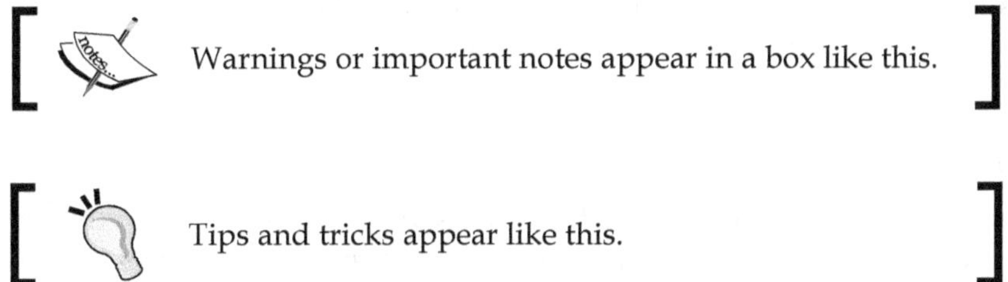

Reader feedback

Feedback from our readers is always welcome. Let us know what you think about this book—what you liked or disliked. Reader feedback is important for us as it helps us develop titles that you will really get the most out of.

To send us general feedback, simply e-mail `feedback@packtpub.com`, and mention the book's title in the subject of your message.

If there is a topic that you have expertise in and you are interested in either writing or contributing to a book, see our author guide at `www.packtpub.com/authors`.

Customer support

Now that you are the proud owner of a Packt book, we have a number of things to help you to get the most from your purchase.

Errata

Although we have taken every care to ensure the accuracy of our content, mistakes do happen. If you find a mistake in one of our books—maybe a mistake in the text or the code—we would be grateful if you could report this to us. By doing so, you can save other readers from frustration and help us improve subsequent versions of this book. If you find any errata, please report them by visiting `http://www.packtpub.com/submit-errata`, selecting your book, clicking on the **Errata Submission Form** link, and entering the details of your errata. Once your errata are verified, your submission will be accepted and the errata will be uploaded to our website or added to any list of existing errata under the Errata section of that title.

To view the previously submitted errata, go to `https://www.packtpub.com/books/content/support` and enter the name of the book in the search field. The required information will appear under the **Errata** section.

Piracy

Piracy of copyrighted material on the Internet is an ongoing problem across all media. At Packt, we take the protection of our copyright and licenses very seriously. If you come across any illegal copies of our works in any form on the Internet, please provide us with the location address or website name immediately so that we can pursue a remedy.

Please contact us at `copyright@packtpub.com` with a link to the suspected pirated material.

We appreciate your help in protecting our authors and our ability to bring you valuable content.

Questions

If you have a problem with any aspect of this book, you can contact us at `questions@packtpub.com`, and we will do our best to address the problem.

1
Moodle in a Nutshell

In this first chapter, we deal with a short background of Moodle and what it does. We will introduce the architectural structure of Moodle and how the different parts work together. We will also go through the steps for installing Moodle on a Linux server and see how to perform ongoing upgrades.

Background of Moodle

Moodle is an open source web-based course management system that is used by organizations, schools, universities, and training companies globally to provide online learning and the online component of blended learning. It is the world's most widely used open source course management system.

Moodle has a large community that collaborates in both developing and using the application through the community forums at `https://moodle.org/`. Moodle HQ has a team of full-time core developers who work on the ongoing support and development of the application. There is a global network of certified Moodle service providers that financially support the Moodle HQ by providing commercial services to organizations who use Moodle.

Moodle was originally released in 2002 by Martin Dougiamas to help teachers take advantage of the online environment to create online courses. Since then, there have been regular releases, with releases coming out on average every 6 months. The project is led and coordinated by Martin at Moodle HQ in Perth, Australia.

Moodle has a modern and easy-to-use interface that works well on desktops and mobile devices.

Users get a customizable dashboard where they can display their course information, calendar, and messages and manage their personal files on the system. Users can manage their own profile to control the level of notifications that they receive from the system, including being able to have forum posts sent out in daily batches.

The course management of Moodle enable easy communication, collaboration, and content creation for teachers and students in addition to comprehensive assessment tools, including the online quiz tool. Teachers can simply create content in Moodle using the accessible text editor or upload files, learning objects, and multimedia into the Moodle course including embedding third-party content such as SlideShare, YouTube, and other social systems into the pages of the course.

Teachers can easily track students' progress through the course content and activities, and students can monitor their own progress, with an understanding of what is left to accomplish.

From an administration perspective, Moodle is very flexible. For example, it has many options available for user authentication and course enrolment due to the many plugins that are available. These offer organizations many approaches to manage how they integrate Moodle into their other systems.

Architecture of Moodle

Moodle stands for Modular Object-Oriented Dynamic Learning Environment, which explains the background to the plugin structure of the Moodle application as it is all modular.

There are many plugin types in Moodle including authentication, enrolment, themes, course formats, and each of these control an aspect of Moodle such as, an authentication plugin, which enables the administrator to control how users log into Moodle.

Moodle is written in PHP and can be run on a number of web servers that support PHP, including Apache and IIS.

Moodle supports a number of database types including MySQL, PostgreSQL, MSSQL, Oracle, and SQLite. However, the most supported and tested would be MySQL and PostgreSQL.

Moodle also stores files in a directory on the server, which is referred to as the `moodledata` directory. Moodle stores all of its files in this directory including temporary files, session data, and user uploaded files.

Always check the minimum server requirements for the version of Moodle that you are planning to install. These are found in the release notes on the MoodleDocs site. The latest version will be found at `https://docs.moodle.org/en/Installing_Moodle#Requirements`.

So, when considering the Moodle installation, you must consider the PHP files, the `moodledata` directory, and the database.

Installing Moodle

We are now going to deal with the specification required for installing Moodle on a Linux server.

Server specifications

Moodle is most typically installed on Linux servers using Apache, MySQL, and PHP, known as the LAMP platform. Hence, this installation combination is the most tried, tested, stable, and supported. This is what we will be using in the coming examples.

Hardware

There is no way to set a requirement for the hardware for a Moodle site without understanding how many users will be using the site and how they will be using it. Moodle is an enterprise system, so be sure that you give it sufficient memory, CPU, and disk space. Active monitoring of the performance can help you identify if more is needed. For the most up-to-date guidance, you should check the Moodle docs, the `https://moodle.org/` forums, or contact a certified Moodle service provider.

For the installation and upgrade examples in this chapter, if you do not have a Linux server at hand, you can use a Linux virtual server from any cloud provider, such as Amazon cloud, Digital Ocean, Linode, or similar. Just be sure to choose an image with an up-to-date LAMP stack that meets the minimum requirements for your Moodle version.

Software

Moodle provides detailed specifications for required software for each Moodle version.

Check out `https://docs.moodle.org/dev/Releases` for further details. For instance, `https://docs.moodle.org/dev/Moodle_2.8_release_notes#Server_requirements` has the 2.8 version list.

Code specifications

We are now going to cover the installing of Moodle, where to download code from (including which version), and the settings that are used to run the installation process.

Moodle download

We always recommend that you download your Moodle code directly from `https://moodle.org/`. The following are the steps for downloading Moodle:

1. Firstly, you need to decide which version of Moodle you wish to install. Here, we will be installing the latest stable version of Moodle 2.8.
2. On your server, locate and go to the directory where you plan to host your moodle site.
3. Then, you can either download the ZIP file from `https://download.moodle.org/` and unzip it, or use Git to pull the code from the Moodle Git repository. We recommend Git for its ease of use, particularly for upgrading, which we shall cover later in this chapter.
4. If using Git, use the following Git command:

   ```
   git clone -b MOODLE_28_STABLE git://git.moodle.org/moodle.git
   ```

5. The resulting directory will be called `moodle`. This directory should be located in your web server directory so that it can be accessed via the Internet.
6. If you need to specify a different directory name, such as `learning`, use the following Git command instead:

   ```
   git clone -b MOODLE_28_STABLE git://git.moodle.org/moodle.git
   learning
   ```

7. Alternatively, if you prefer to not have a subdirectory called `moodle`, move all of the contents directly into your web server directory.

File permissions

You need to make the moodle files secure as they are publically accessible via the Internet.

Ensure that all moodle files are owned by the root user and are only readable by the web server user as follows:

```
chown -R root /path/to/moodle
chmod -R 0755 /path/to/moodle
```

Database setup

Next, in your designated database, you need to set up an empty database and a dedicated user with sufficient access.

For instance, in MySQL, the following mysql command line queries would suffice:

```
CREATE DATABASE <databasename> DEFAULT CHARACTER SET utf8 COLLATE utf8_
unicode_ci;

GRANT SELECT,INSERT,UPDATE,DELETE,CREATE,CREATE TEMPORARY
TABLES,DROP,INDEX,ALTER ON <databasename>.* TO <username>@<dbhost>
IDENTIFIED BY '<password>';
```

You should not use the database root or admin account for security reasons.

You will need to take note of the following details for the installation process later:

- dbhost: This is usually localhost, if on the same server as the Moodle site.
- dbname: This is the name of the empty database.
- dbuser: This is the username for the dedicated user.
- dbpass: This is the password for the dedicated user.

Moodledata directory setup

You will also need to set up a dedicated file directory to hold all of the moodle files.

This moodledata directory cannot be located within the moodle web directory or within the web server directory as otherwise this would be a security risk.

However, the web server needs write access to the moodledata directory as browser actions will generate data file creation, editing, and deletion.

Hence, use the following command lines in a suitable server directory:

```
mkdir <moodledatadirectoryname>

chmod -R 0777 /path/to/moodledatadirectory
```

Moodle installer

The moodle installer can be run in two ways:

- Command line installer
- Web installer

If running the command-line installer, it's advisable to run it as the web server user, for instance `www-data` for Ubuntu/Debian or `apache` for Centos.

Hence:

```
chown www-data /path/to/moodle
cd /path/to/moodle/admin/cli
sudo -u www-data /usr/bin/php install.php
chown -R root /path/to/moodle
```

The main configuration settings are the URL, the directory path to both the moodle code files and the `moodledata` files, and the database details. If in doubt, use the default settings and remember that these settings can be easily edited after the installation process if needed in the `/path/to/moodle/config.php` file. You will also need to supply an administrator account username with a secure password, which you need to retain permanently. If you lose this, it can be changed from the command line if required.

To run the web installer instead, go to your Moodle site's main URL within your browser and submit the same configuration settings as for the command-line version. Once the installer has finished, you will have access to your Moodle site.

Essential configurations

After the actual code and database installation, there are a number of systems that need to be configured to ensure the Moodle site is operating correctly. These are as follows:

- Email
- System paths
- Cron

Email settings

Navigate to **Administration** | **Site administration** | **Plugins** | **Message Outputs** | **Email**.

Enter and save your SMTP settings as required to ensure that Moodle is able to send out e-mails. This is essential for functions such as email-based self-registration:

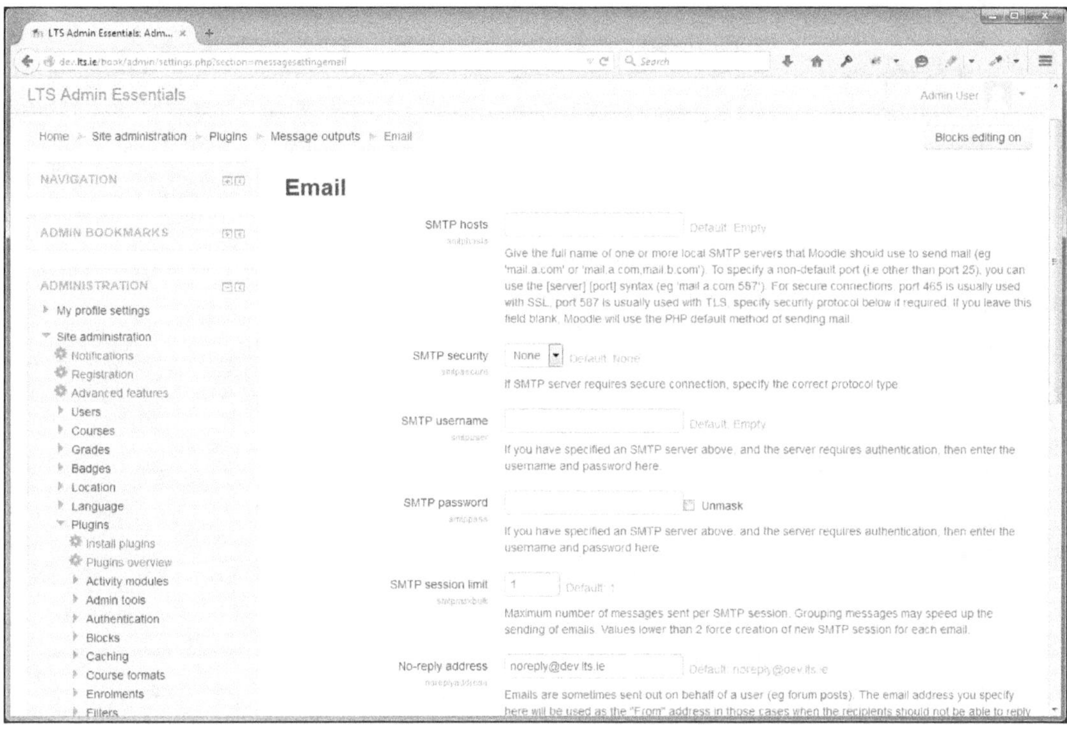

System paths

Navigate to **Administration** | **Site administration** | **Server** | **System paths**.

Enter and save your specified paths to ghostscript, du, aspell, and dot binaries:

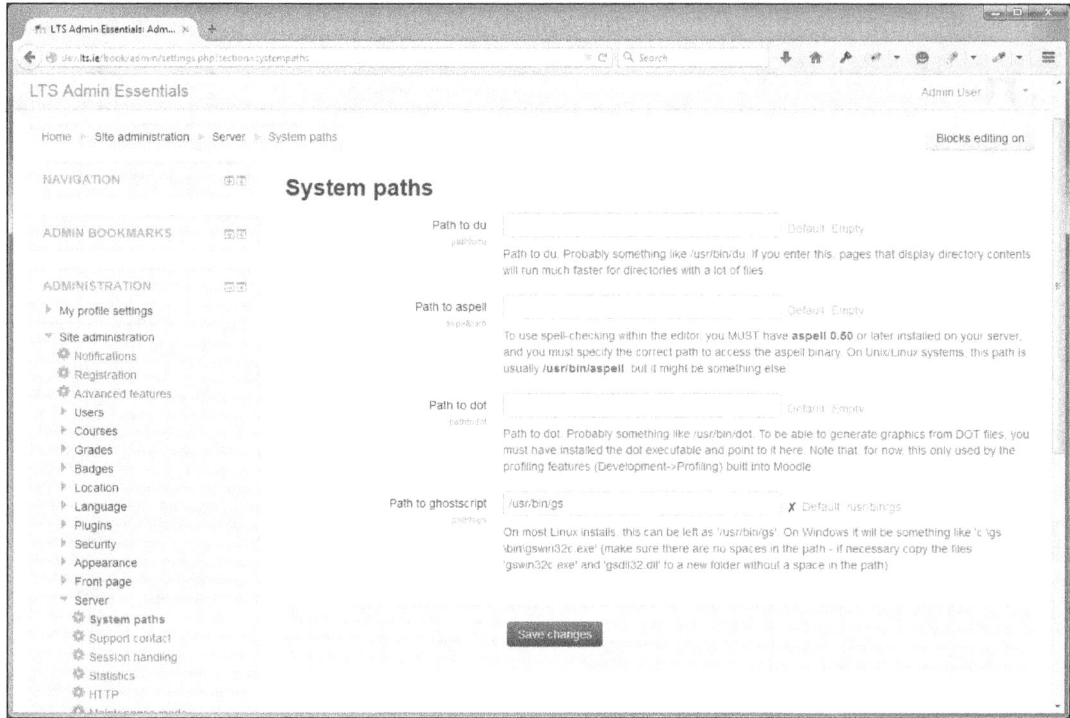

Cron

Cron is essential to the processing of many Moodle background functions.

The moodle cron script is located at `/path/to/moodle/admin/cli/cron.php`.

This cron script needs to be scheduled in the server's own cron program for UNIX or Linux.

For instance, on Ubuntu/Debian servers, to edit the cron program:

1. Use the command line:

   ```
   crontab -u www-data -e
   ```

2. Do normal edits with standard vi commands.

3. Add the line to the crontab:

```
*/1 * * * * /usr/bin/php /path/to/moodle/
  admin/cli/cron.php >/dev/null
```

4. Adjust the exact time configuration as required, the above example runs once every minute.
5. Alternatively, use this line to log the cron results for tracking, please note, this file will get very large.

```
*/1 * * * * /usr/bin/php /path/to/moodle/admin/cli/
  cron.php >> /path/to/moodledata/temp/cron.log 2>&1
```

6. Then do *Ctrl* + *O*, to write, and then *Ctrl* + *X* to exit.
7. The cron program will now be updated.

Updating Moodle

As mentioned earlier, Moodle HQ releases updates on a regular basis, which include bug fixes and security patches. Hence, it is important to know how to update the Moodle codebase to keep it secure.

Upgrading from one version to another

> Most importantly, any Moodle site older than 2.2 being upgraded to above 2.2 must be first upgraded to 2.2 completely, and then upgraded to 2.X.

Your first step is to create a copy of your live site and practice the upgrade process on it from the beginning to the end, ensuring that everything upgrades as expected.

Cloning your Moodle site

These are the recommended steps to create a clone of your Moodle live site:

1. **Moodle code directory**: Create a brand new directory and fully copy all directories and files from the live moodle code directory into it, following the installation guidelines for its location and permissions.
2. **Moodle data directory**: Create a brand new moodledata folder, again following the installation guidelines for its location and permissions.

3. **Database**: The following are the steps to create a new database:
    1. Create a new database in your database application, again following the installation guidelines.
    2. Create a new database user with relevant permissions to the new database, again following the installation guidelines.
    3. Populate the new database from a full MySQL or other database dump file of the live Moodle database.
    4. For instance, to create a MySQL dump in normal command line:

       ```
       mysqldump -h localhost -u <dbuser> --password=<dbpass>
         -C -Q -e --create-options <dbname> > dbnameclone.sql
       ```

    5. This also requires you to ensure correct character encoding is used if needed as a MySQL dump is not 100% reliable for all UTF-8 encoding.
    6. To populate the new database with the dump file:
    7. Check you are in the correct new database in MySQL command line and only then use the following query:

       ```
       source dbnameclone.sql;
       ```

4. **Config.php**: This urgently needs to be changed so edit this in the new moodle code directory to point to the new moodledata directory, the new database, and the new URL as it will initially have the settings to the live site, which urgently needs to be changed.
5. The cloned site should now be operational.
6. **Login**: Check that the clone site is accessible.
7. Upload a file resource to check that the moodledata directory permissions and locations are all working correctly.
8. Review a course and check that it appears as it should.
9. Update your user profile with a minor change and check that the new values are in the new database, not the live database.
10. There is also an admin tool on your Moodle site to find and replace any potential hard-coded URLs for resources such as images. This is located at `admin/tool/replace/index.php`. Please note that this will only work on sites, which use either MySQL or Postgres.

The following upgrade steps should, therefore, be run firstly and completely on your cloned site and only then on your live site.

Upgrade preparation

Put your site into maintenance mode by navigating to **Administration** | **Site administration** | **Server** | **Maintenance mode**. This prevents non-admin users from logging into the site and altering any of its contents, such as course resources, submitting assignments, posting to forums, and so on.

Any of these types of alterations will not only render your backups obsolete, but also compromise the integrity of the final upgraded site.

Before you start any upgrades, you need to take a full backup of your Moodle site. This involves three components:

- moodle code directory: This may contain external plugins and other customized changes to core Moodle
- moodledata directory: This contains all stored moodle data files, which the Moodle code relies on for course resources, log files, and so on
- moodle database: This contains all database records related to the Moodle site

Moodle code directory

Take a full backup of this directory and also have a list of all external plugins and any core code customizations, which have been implemented.

Moodle data directory

Take a full backup of this directory. Its location is found in the `config.php` script.

Moodle database

Take a full MySQL dump of the relevant Moodle database. This also requires you to ensure correct character encoding used if needed as the MySQL dump is not 100 percent reliable for all UTF-8 encoding.

Moodle download

As with an initial Moodle installation, we always recommend that you download your Moodle code directly from `https://moodle.org/`. For this example, we will be updating to Moodle Version 2.8.

You can either download the ZIP file from https://download.moodle.org/ and unzip it, or use Git to pull the code from the Moodle Git repository.

1. First of all, on your server, locate and go to the directory containing the moodle site directory which you are upgrading.
2. Download and unzip the ZIP file from https://moodle.org/ or use the following Git command (for versions other than 2.8, use the relevant branch name):

```
git clone -b MOODLE_28_STABLE git://git.moodle.org/moodle.git
<directory>
```

Please note that this will overwrite the existing data in the target moodle code directory with the latest 2.8 moodle code.

Once you have completed the updating of the Moodle code directory, you then need to complete the following steps:

1. Where external plugins have more up-to-date code for your upgrade version, replace the older plugin code completely, which is explained more in *Chapter 6, Managing Site Plugins*.
2. Where you have made previous customizations to core Moodle code (which is not a recommended practice for this exact reason!), you will need to locate each file in turn and manually add the customized code into them.
3. Copy the config.php script from the backup into the target moodle code directory.
4. Check that all the moodle code directories, subdirectories, and files are web server readable.
5. Check that your usual cron usage is enabled, either that the admin/cron.php script is executable via the browser or more typically that the site is listed in the cron program for your server, which is explained more in *Chapter 8, Miscellaneous Admin Tasks*.

6. Go to the notifications page by navigating to **Administration** | **Site administration** | **Notifications** to kick off the final upgrade process and click on **Continue**:

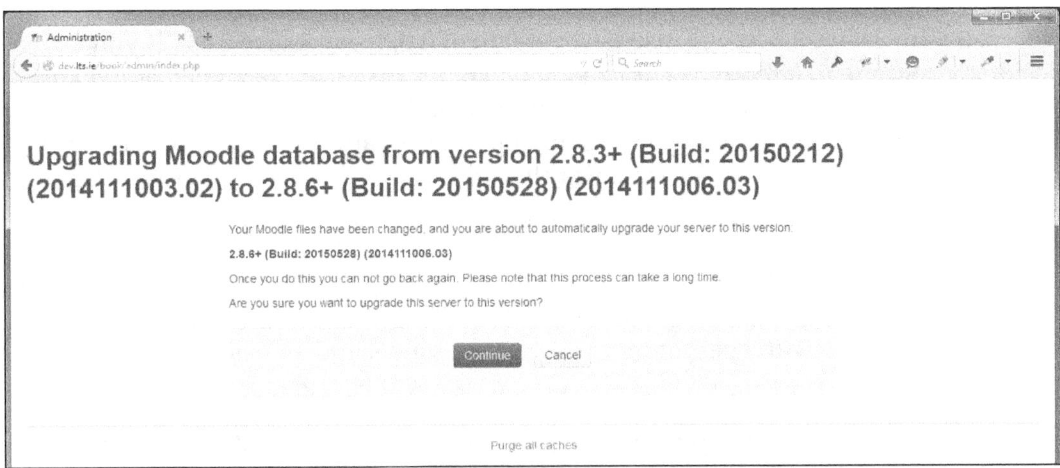

7. Once the upgrade process has been completed, purge all caches by navigating to **Administration** | **Site administration** | **Development** | **Purge all caches**. This will ensure that the browser displays the latest Moodle site and not any cached information.
8. Test the site fully according to your organization's requirements. We would suggest at a minimum:
    1. Login as Admin, teacher, and student
    2. Upload a file resource
    3. Review a course and its contents
    4. Update your user profile
9. Take your site out of maintenance mode, if previously enabled, by navigating to **Administration** | **Site administration** | **Server** | **Maintenance mode**.

Maintaining the version code

Each Moodle version branch is updated weekly to ensure that all code is up-to-date, which may include fixes to recently discovered issues.

Hence, if your site is 2.8, it will also be a version of 2.8, for instance 2.8.3. If you decide to upgrade to a more recent version of 2.8, for instance 2.8.6, you should still follow the exact same procedure as we explained earlier for the upgrade process. This ensures that if there are any issues during the upgrade process, you have an easily accessible original version to instantly roll back to.

When to update

Moodle has minor releases every 2 months and major releases every 6 months. It is advisable to update with every minor release if possible, and at least yearly with a major release.

There is also a long-term support release (currently 2.7 and the next one is 3.0) that can offer the opportunity to only do a major update every 3 years.

Summary

In this chapter, we looked at the background of Moodle, its architecture, and the installation and upgrade process.

In the next chapter, we will look at the essential areas of user account management, creating users, editing users, and customizing user details as required.

2
Managing User Accounts and Authentication

Administrators can perform a wide range of tasks related to user accounts on the Moodle site. These tasks include creating users, editing users, defining cohorts (groups of users for help in enrolment process), and customizing the user profile with user pictures and extra fields.

In the first chapter, we looked at Moodle, the architecture, and the installation process. Once installed, the administrator needs to configure how users are added, edited, and managed within Moodle.

In this chapter, we deal with the essential areas of user account management that every administrator will have to deal with:

- Add a new user
- Upload users
- User authentication
- Tackle the common choices of user authentication:
    - Manual authentication
    - E-mail-based self-registration

Creating users

To create a user in Moodle:

1. Log in as an administrator level user account.
2. Access the user management options in the **Administration** block under **Site administration** | **Users** | **Accounts**.

3. Click on **Add a new user**. This brings up the following page:

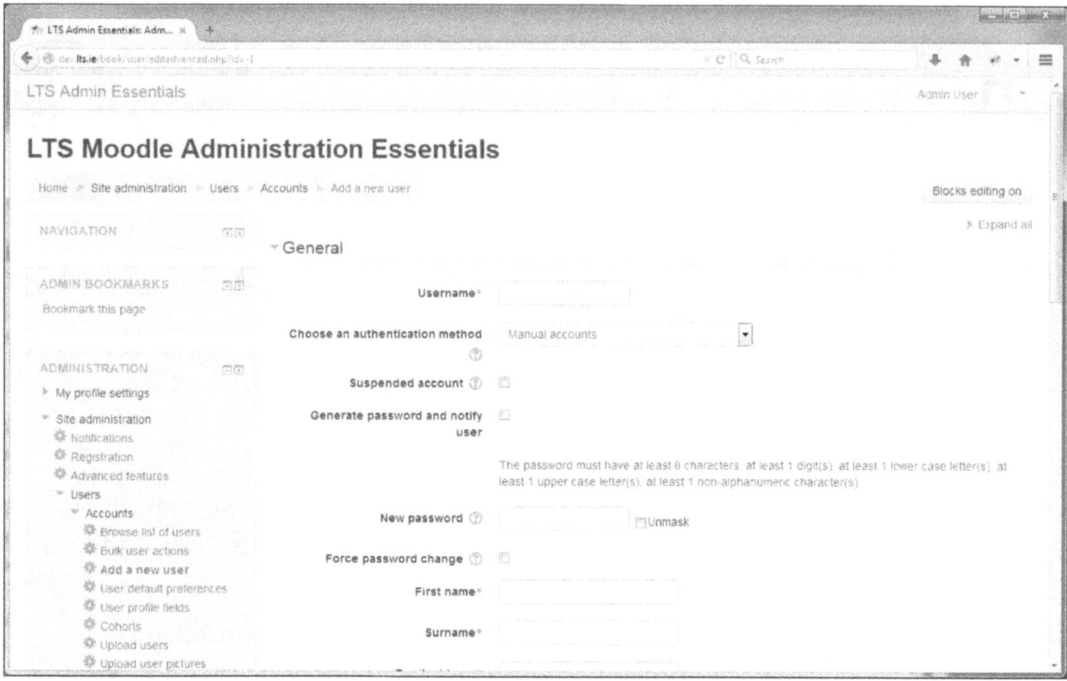

4. To fill in the **Username**, use the person's first name and last name with no spaces and all in lowercase for the username.
5. The **username** column must be all lowercase using letters, numbers, and any of the following characters: hyphen "-", underscore "_", period ".", or an at character "@".
6. If you are creating an account for a user with external authentication, then select the relevant option for the **Authentication method**, otherwise leave the **Authentication method** to `Manual Accounts`.

External authentication is where Moodle connects to a different system, such as Microsoft Active Directory, to authenticate the users. There are a number of such systems supported by Moodle.

7. Create a secure password for the user and enter it into the **New password** field.

Passwords must adhere to the password policy in Moodle, configured in site policies section, which by default include one uppercase letter, one lowercase letter, one number, and one non-alphanumeric. It must be at least eight characters long.

8. Enter their first name into the **First name** field.
9. Enter their Surname into the **Surname** field.
10. Enter their e-mail into the **Email address** field.
11. Select the preference for the **Email digest type** setting which are as follows:
    - **No digest (single email per forum post)**.
    - **Complete (daily email with full posts)** (that is all content).
    - **Subjects (daily email with subjects only)** (recommended).
12. Select the preference for the **Forum auto-subscribe** setting.
    - **Yes: when I post, subscribe me to that forum discussion** (recommended).
    - **No: don't automatically subscribe me to forums discussion**.
13. Enter the text for the user's location in the **City/town** field.
14. Select the correct country under **Select a country**.
15. Select the timezone for the **Timezone** setting, if you know the user's timezone.
16. Select the language in the **Preferred language** menu if needed.

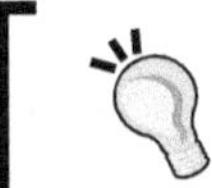

There are other user profile fields that can be filled in, but we have only covered what we believe are the most essential here.

17. Carefully check all entries to make sure you have no mistakes, such as typos.
18. Click on the **Create user** button to save all changes.
19. The new user account is created in Moodle, but as you created the username and password yourself, you will need to give these to the user.
20. The account will now be able to log into the site. However, it will not have any permissions yet in any courses, either as a student, course creator, or teacher as this is a separate action.

This area of enrolment is handled later in *Chapter 5, Role Management*.

Editing a user

A common task that administrators undertake is editing an existing user profile and changing details, such as their password or e-mail. The first step is to use the filters to search for the user that you want to edit.

Searching for a user account

1. Navigate to **Administration** | **Site-Administration** | **Users** | **Accounts** | **Browse list of users**.
2. Type the user's name or portion of their name into the **User full name** field:

3. Click on **Add filter**. This will display the list of users that have the text in their full name.
4. To edit the user account, click on the cogwheel icon to the right-hand side of the user record. This brings up the user account editing page, as follows:

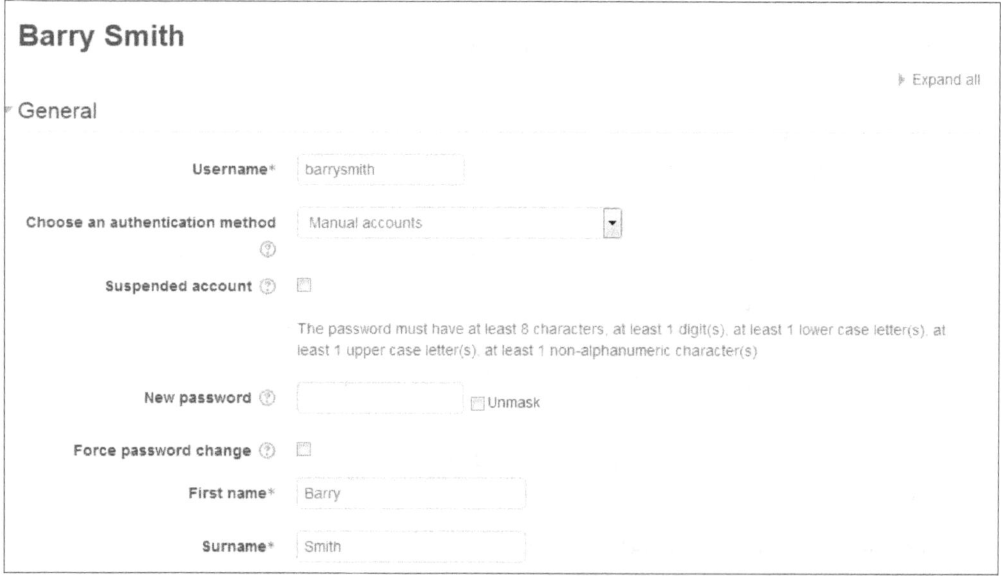

Editing the user account

This process is the same for an administrator editing a user account and a user editing their own account with some exceptions not being available to the end user.

The administrator can change the username, authentication method, and password for a user, using the following options. Be sure to notify the user of any changes:

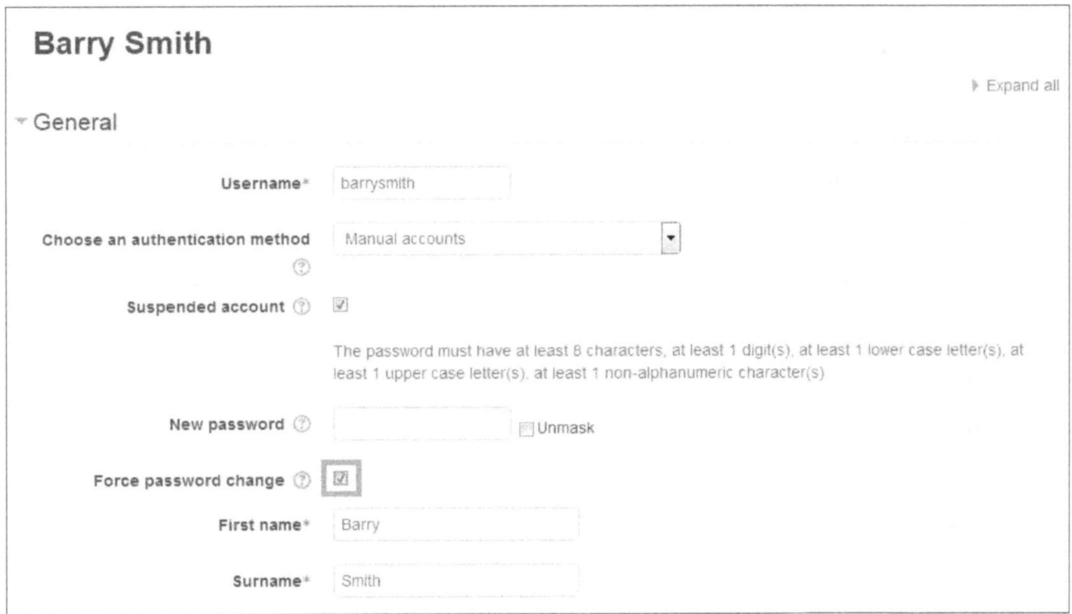

It is good practice to force the user to change their own password after you issue them one, and this can be achieved by ticking the **Force password change** checkbox.

It is also possible to suspend the user account, which stops them from logging in, by ticking the **Suspended account** checkbox.

The administrator can then change any of the normal account details that a user can configure, including:

- First name
- Surname
- Email address
- Email display
- Email format
- Email digest type

- Forum auto-subscribe
- Forum tracking
- When editing text
- Screen Reader
- City/town
- Country
- Timezone
- Preferred language
- Description
- User Picture
- Interests

There are also the optional fields that include:

- Web Page
- ICQ number
- Skype ID
- AIM ID
- Yahoo ID
- MSN ID
- ID number
- Institution
- Department
- Phone
- Mobile Phone
- Address

If you added any custom profile fields, they will appear on this editing page as well.

Custom profile fields are extra fields that an administrator can add to all user account profiles. These can be used for organization-specific information, such as managers' name, office location, or emergency contact information, and can be hidden from others looking at the profile.

After completing the editing, click on the **Update profile** button to save all changes.

Uploading users

An administrator can bulk upload users in Moodle using a spreadsheet. This can be created in Excel, Open Office, or a similar application like Google Docs. In this section, we will refer to using Microsoft Excel.

The minimum information that is required as data in the spreadsheet includes the first name, last name, e-mail, username, and password. The password is not mandatory, and if you leave it blank, it will autogenerate the password and send an e-mail to the user immediately with their username and password.

Preparing the spreadsheet

To prepare your file for uploading perform the following:

1. Open Microsoft Excel.
2. Create five column names in the first row as the following – these should be lowercase and no spaces:
   - `username`
   - `password`
   - `firstname`
   - `lastname`
   - `email`
3. Fill in the user details:

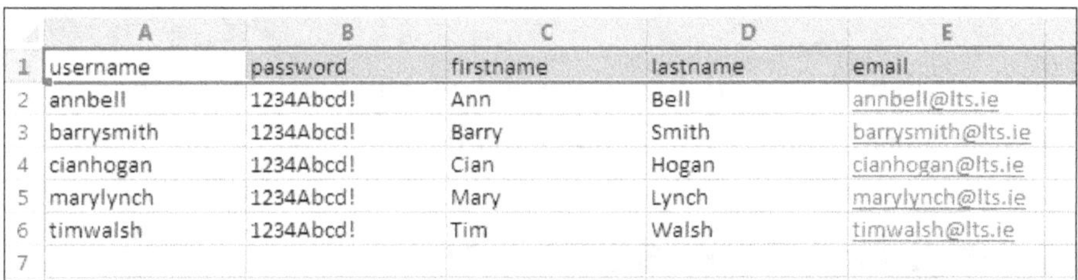

	A	B	C	D	E
1	username	password	firstname	lastname	email
2	annbell	1234Abcd!	Ann	Bell	annbell@lts.ie
3	barrysmith	1234Abcd!	Barry	Smith	barrysmith@lts.ie
4	cianhogan	1234Abcd!	Cian	Hogan	cianhogan@lts.ie
5	marylynch	1234Abcd!	Mary	Lynch	marylynch@lts.ie
6	timwalsh	1234Abcd!	Tim	Walsh	timwalsh@lts.ie
7					

4. For the username, we suggest you use the first name and last name with no spaces, no special characters, and all lowercase or e-mail address in lowercase.

5. If you are creating manual accounts, you can set a password if you prefer, otherwise if you leave it blank, Moodle will send the user their username and password via e-mail after the upload.
6. Enter their first name and their last name—be sure to avoid special characters in the fields like quotes or commas.
7. Enter their e-mail address.
8. Repeat this process for all the users that you want to create.
9. Under the File menu, select **Save As**. Then, select `CSV (Comma delimited)` (`*.csv`) for **Save as type**:

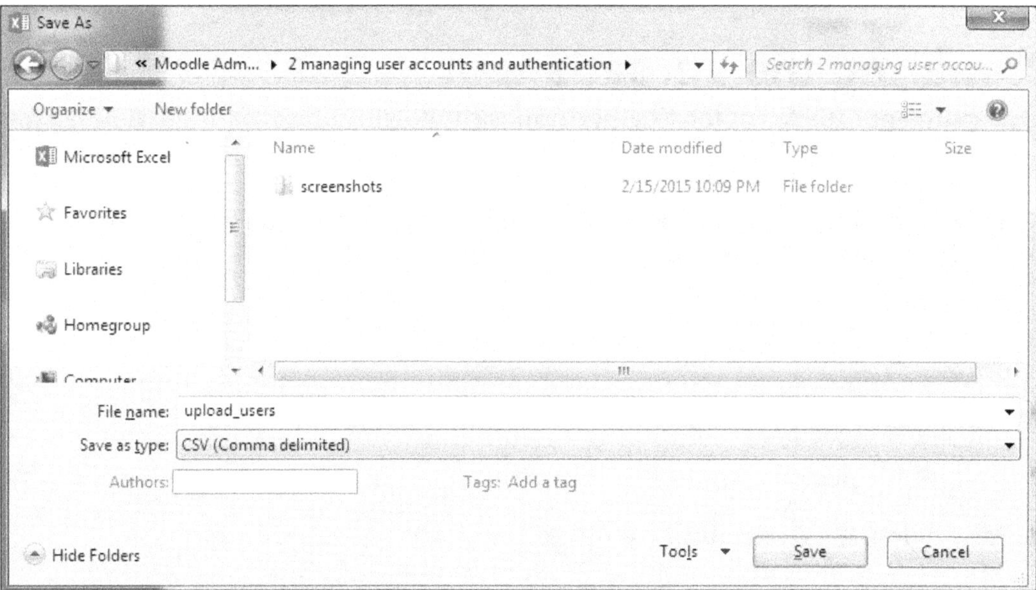

10. Click on **Save**. Excel will give you a warning about the format.
11. Click on **Yes** to continue to save the `csv` file.

Uploading the spreadsheet

The following are the steps for uploading the spreadsheet:

1. Log in as an administrator user account.
2. Access the user management options in the **Administration** block by navigating to **Site administration** | **Users** | **Accounts**.

3. Click on **Upload users**:

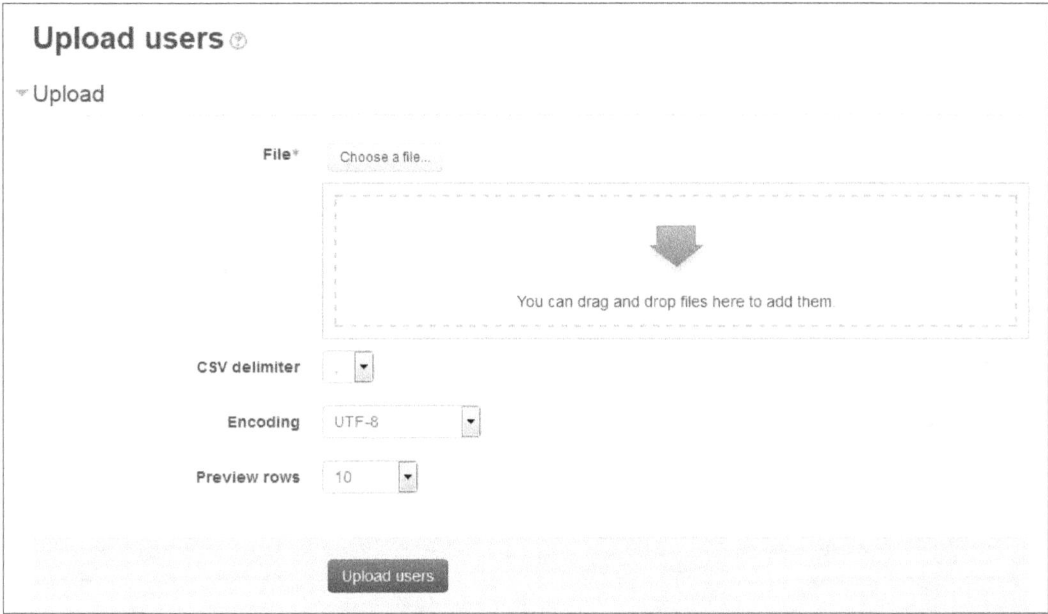

4. Click on **Choose a file** to bring up the file picker.
5. Click on **Upload a file** and then click on **Browse**.
6. Find the file on your computer, and then click on **Open** to select it.
7. Click on **Upload this file**.
8. Change the **Preview rows** setting to a larger suitable number if you are uploading a lot of users. This will enable you to preview that their details have been interpreted correctly.
9. Click on **Upload users**. This will bring up the preview page before actually creating the accounts.

10. Check the **Upload users preview** details of the users are correct:

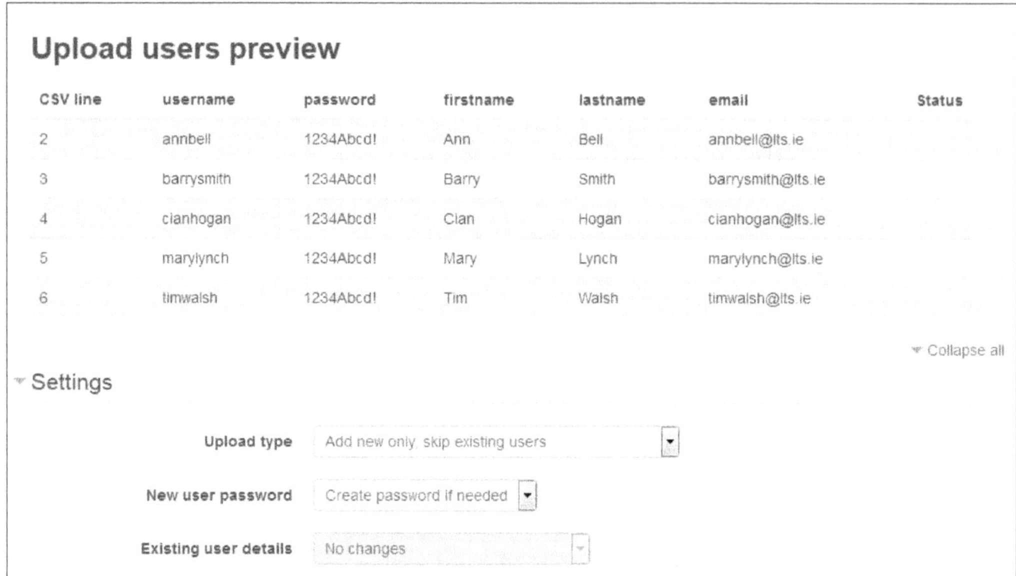

11. Under **Settings** | **Upload Type**.
12. If you are creating new users, select **Add new only, skip existing users**.
13. Select **Update existing users** only if you are updating existing users. Note that if you have set passwords in the spreadsheet, you will overwrite their password if they changed it. This does not matter for users with external authentication, as it is not used.
14. Select **Add new and update existing users** if you are creating new users and updating existing ones.

15. Under default values, click on **Show more...** to see all the options:

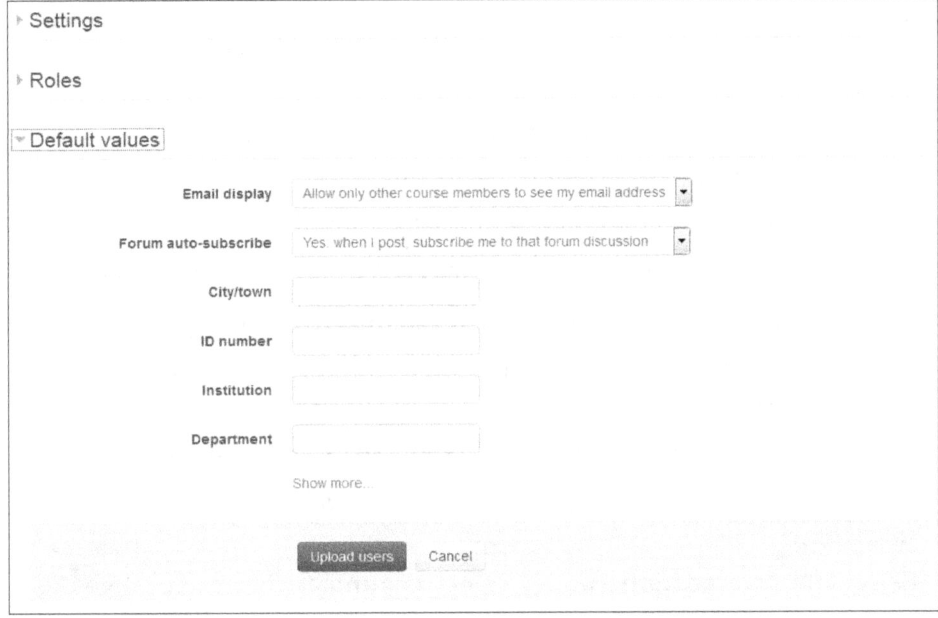

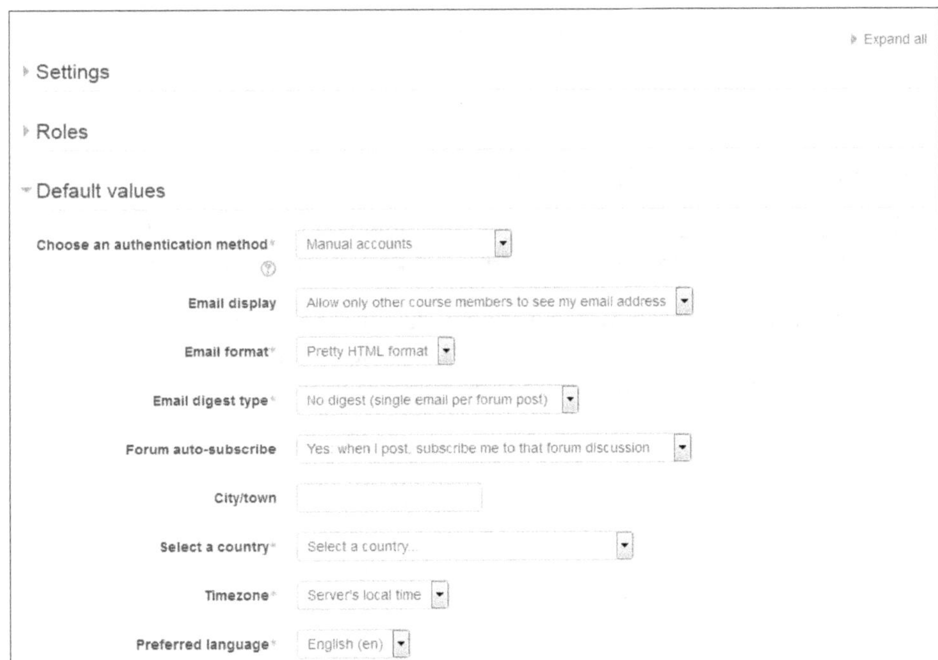

16. For the **New user password** field, one option is to leave it as **Create password if needed**. Then Moodle will generate a password if none is supplied in the `CSV` file. The other option is to set it to **Field required in file**. Hence, Moodle will require the password column to be present and not empty for each user.
17. Select the preference for the **Email digest type** setting:
    - **No digest (single email per forum post)**
    - **Complete (daily email with full posts)** (that is all content)
    - **Subjects (daily email with subjects only)** (recommended)
18. Select the preference for the **Forum auto-subscribe** setting:
    - **Yes: when I post, subscribe me to that forum discussion** (recommended)
    - **No: don't automatically subscribe me to forums discussions**
19. Enter the text for the users' location in the **City/town** field. Users can change this later.
20. Select the correct country under **Select a country**. They can change this later.
21. Select the timezone for the **Timezone** setting if you know the users' timezone.
22. Select the language in the **Preferred language** menu if needed.
23. Click on the **Upload users** button to save all changes.

User authentication

User authentication handles how a user profile logs into Moodle. Each user typically will have a username and password that they will enter into the login form.

When they submit the login form, Moodle determines if they are a user and how they should be authenticated as a valid user. To achieve this, every Moodle user account is designated an authentication type.

Authentication types

When a user attempts to log into Moodle, their authentication type will determine how Moodle authenticates their submitted data (their username and password).

The two most widely used authentication types are Manual accounts and e-mail-based self-registration, which will be described in more detail here.

The most commonly used authentication types are:

- Internal
    - Manual accounts
    - E-mail-based self-registration
- External
    - LDAP
    - External database
    - IMAP

In this section, we will just focus on the two internal authentication types.

How to enable authentication plugins

To configure the available authentication types on a Moodle site, you need to be logged in as administrator.

By default, the two internal plugins Manual accounts and e-mail-based self-registration are enabled. Others can be enabled as required by the organization.

To manage the authentication plugins:

1. Navigate to **Administration** | **Site Administration** | **Plugins** | **Authentication** | **Manage authentication**:

Manage authentication

Available authentication plugins

Name	Users	Enable	Up/Down	Settings	Test settings	Uninstall
Manual accounts	2			Settings		
No login	0			Settings		
Email-based self-registration	0			Settings		Uninstall
CAS server (SSO)	0			Settings		Uninstall
External database	0			Settings	Test settings	Uninstall
FirstClass server	0			Settings		Uninstall
IMAP server	0			Settings		Uninstall
LDAP server	0			Settings		
MNet authentication	0			Settings		
NNTP server	0			Settings		Uninstall
No authentication	0			Settings		Uninstall
PAM (Pluggable Authentication Modules)	0			Settings		Uninstall
POP3 server	0			Settings		Uninstall

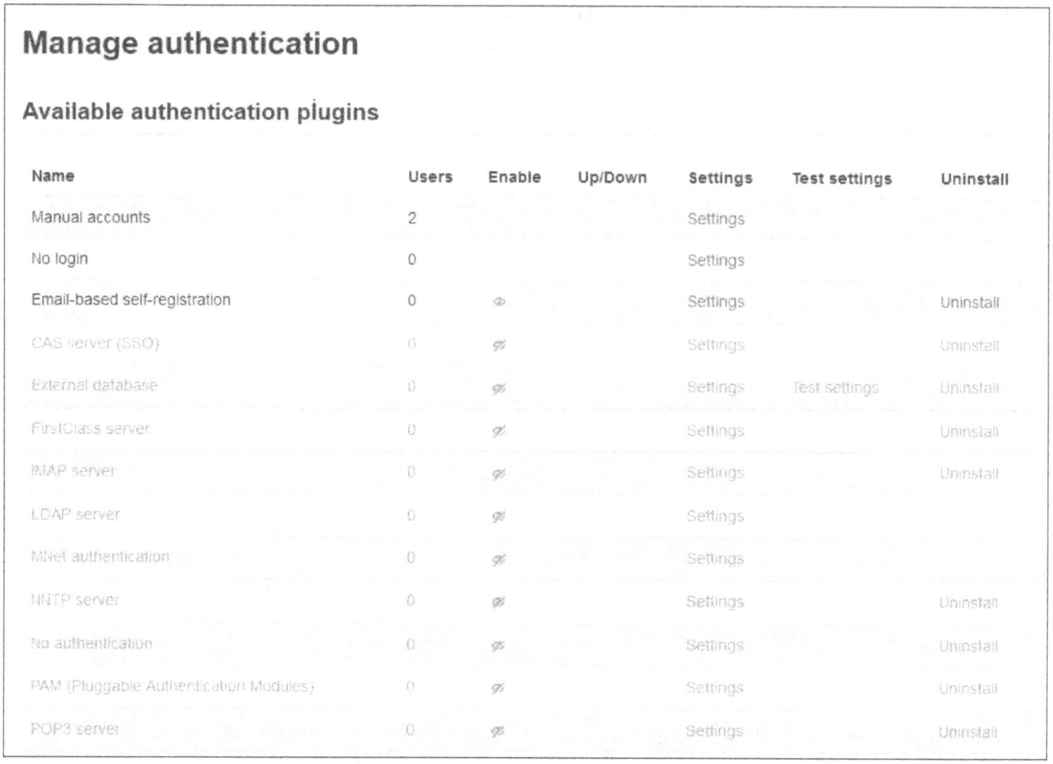

2. Click on the **Enable** column icon to alter each plugin's status to enable or disable as required. This icon usually looks like an open eyeball when enabled.

The **Common settings** section is visible as you scroll further down the page. This section includes options such as:

- **Self registration**: This defaults to disable, and is needed for e-mail-based self-registration.
- **Guest login button**: This defaults to show.
- **ReCAPTCHA deployment**: This is advised for e-mail-based self-registration to reduce spam.

Authentication configuration for a single user creation

When a user is added via the interface as a single user, their authentication type defaults to **Manual accounts**.

Navigate to **Administration** | **Site Administration** | **Users** | **Accounts** | **Add a new user**.

In the **Add User** form, the **Choose an authentication method** dropdown will allow you to select one from the available authentication types. As mentioned, it defaults to **Manual accounts**:

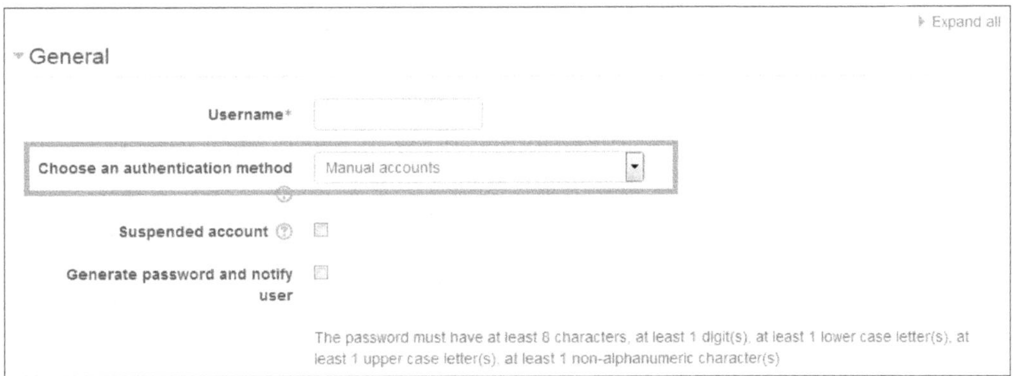

Authentication configuration for the CSV file user upload

When a CSV file of users is added via the interface, the authentication type defaults to **Manual accounts**. This can be changed to any of the other active authentication types.

1. Navigate to **Administration** | **Site Administration** | **Users** | **Accounts** | **Upload users**.
2. In the **Upload users** form, select the CSV file of users you wish to upload. Change any of the other form options as required, and click on **Upload users**.
3. In the **Upload users preview** form, you need to expand the **Default** values section. If not expanded, then click on the **Show more...** link.

4. The **Choose an authentication method** dropdown will now display, to allow you to select one from the available authentication types. It defaults to **Manual accounts**.

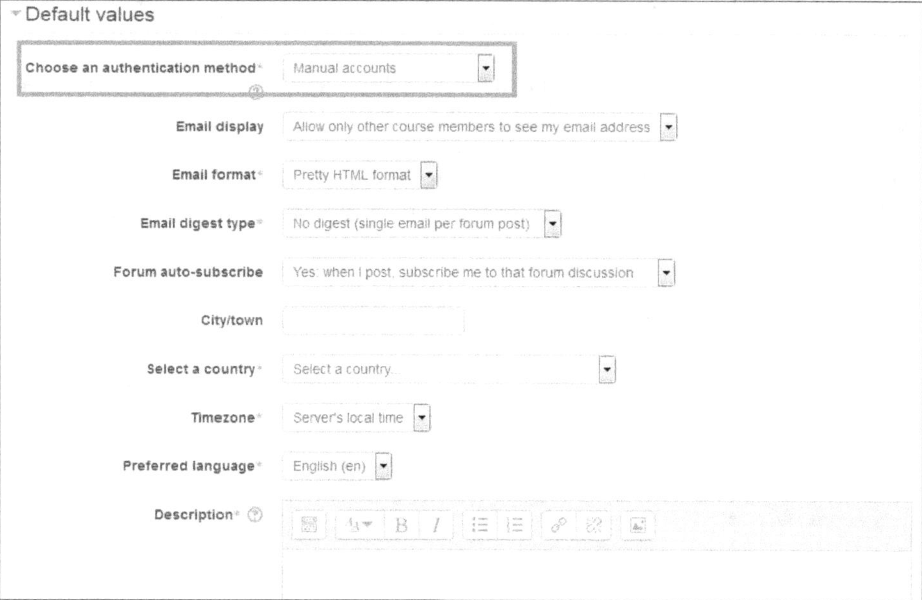

Manual authentication

When a user attempts to log into Moodle with an authentication type of **Manual accounts**, their submitted login details will be compared with the username and password found in the Moodle user database. If validated, the user will then be allowed access to the Moodle site.

[The password is not stored in the database as plain text, so it cannot be retrieved later, only changed.]

The optional configuration

The manual accounts authentication has a number of options that can be configured as follows:

1. Navigate to **Administration** | **Site Administration** | **Plugins** | **Authentication** | **Manual accounts**.
2. **Enable Password expiry** defaults to **No**.

3. **Password duration** (expiry time), to notify users when the password will expire.
4. Lock specific user fields, which prevents users from changing them. For instance, their first name, last name, and e-mail need to remain the same for identification purposes.
5. Change the settings as required and click on **Save changes**:

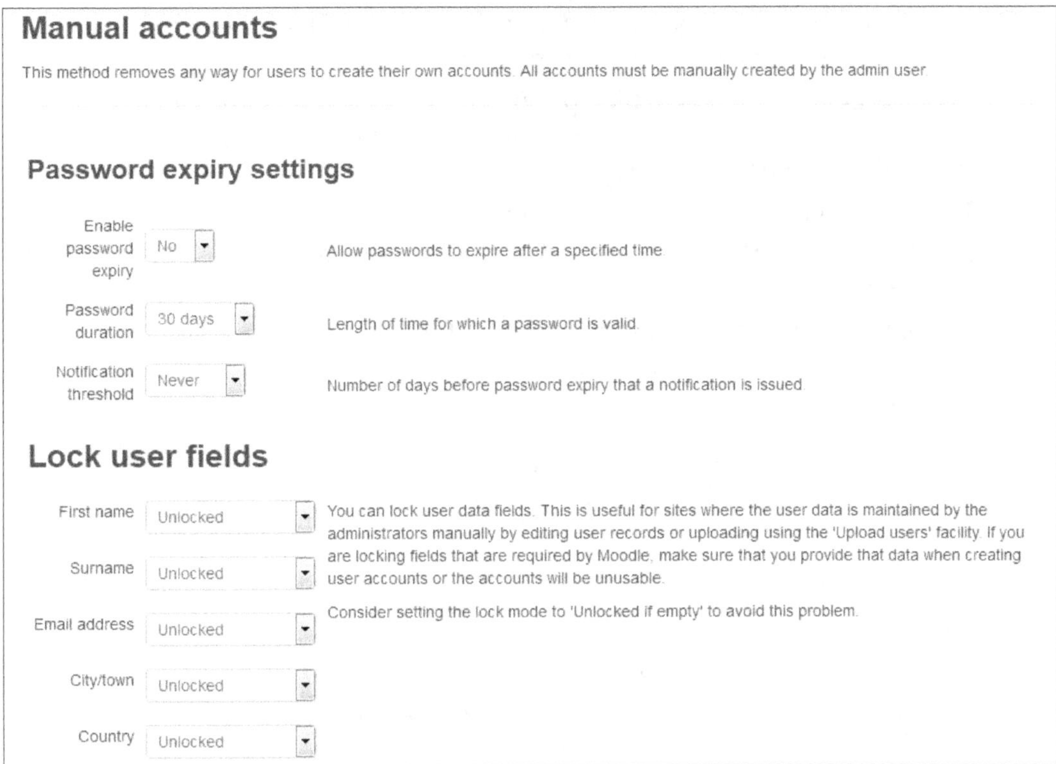

Email-based self-registration authentication

When e-mail-based self-registration is enabled on the Moodle site, it allows anyone with access to the site to register on the site by submitting their own details, depending on a valid e-mail, as this will be used to send a confirmation e-mail to the user to confirm and complete their account creation. Users that do not complete the confirmation process cannot log in.

Once the user has successfully completed their account creation, their subsequent login attempts will be compared in the same manner as manual accounts users, from the username and password found in the Moodle user database.

The optional configuration

The e-mail-based self-registration authentication has a number of options that can be configured:

1. Navigate to **Administration** | **Site Administration** | **Plugins** | **Authentication** | **Email-based self-registration**.
2. **Enable reCAPTCHA element** defaults to **No**. This is highly recommended to reduce spam. For more information on reCAPTCHA, go to `http://www.google.com/recaptcha/intro/index.html`.
3. Lock specific user fields, which prevents users from changing them. For instance, their first name, last name, and e-mail need to remain the same for identification purposes.
4. If you are locking fields that are required by Moodle, make sure that you provide that data when creating user accounts, or the accounts will be unusable.
5. Change the settings as required and click on **Save changes**.

Email-based self-registration

Email-based self-registration enables a user to create their own account via a 'Create new account' button on the login page. The user then receives an email containing a secure link to a page where they can confirm their account. Future logins just check the username and password against the stored values in the Moodle database.

Note: In addition to enabling the plugin, email-based self-registration must also be selected from the self registration drop-down menu on the 'Manage authentication' page.

Settings

Enable reCAPTCHA element: No

Adds a visual/audio confirmation form element to the signup page for email self-registering users. This protects your site against spammers and contributes to a worthwhile cause. See http://www.google.com/recaptcha/learnmore for more details.
PHP cURL extension is required.

Lock user fields

First name: Unlocked
Surname: Unlocked
Email address: Unlocked
City/town: Unlocked
Country: Unlocked

You can lock user data fields. This is useful for sites where the user data is maintained by the administrators manually by editing user records or uploading using the 'Upload users' facility. If you are locking fields that are required by Moodle, make sure that you provide that data when creating user accounts or the accounts will be unusable.

Consider setting the lock mode to 'Unlocked if empty' to avoid this problem.

Summary

In this chapter, we looked at the core administrator roles of user management in adding users, editing users, and bulk uploading users. We also looked at the most common user authentication types and how to configure them.

In the next chapter, we move beyond users into the site structure with categories and courses.

3
Managing Categories and Courses

In the previous chapter, we looked at how to add and manage users on the Moodle site. Once registered, these users need to be enrolled into courses that allow them access to the course content. Setting up courses and organizing them in categories is the next step for administrators.

The structure of the Moodle site from the perspective of teachers and students is defined by the category and course structure. Categories are containers for courses and other categories. You can have categories and subcategories going down as many levels as you need. Courses are placed in categories, at any level, in this structure.

An example of a category structure could be where the year is the top level category, with each course appearing as a subcategory, and each module being an individual Moodle course in that category:

Administrators, course creators, or managers can perform a wide range of tasks relating to categories and courses in the Moodle site.

In this chapter, we deal with the essential areas of category and course management that every administrator will have to deal with:

- Add a new category
- Add a new course
- Upload courses
- Course templates

Category creation

To create a category in Moodle:

1. Log in as an administrator-level user account.
2. Access the category management options in the **Administration** block by navigating to **Site administration** | **Courses** | **Add a category**.
3. Click on **Add a category**. This brings up the following page.

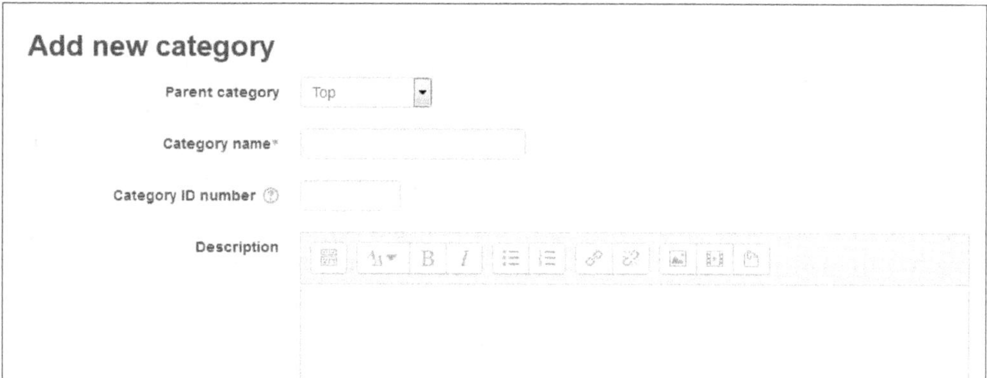

4. Select the **Parent category** from the current existing categories.
5. Fill in the **Category name**. This should be a meaningful name.
6. Enter a **Category ID number** if required for identification purposes.
7. Enter **Description** if required.
8. Click on the **Create category** button to save all changes.

The new category is now created in Moodle.

Course and category management

The overall category hierarchy can be managed by editing category settings. Categories can also be hidden from view as can individual courses, although they can still be seen by administrator level users. Normal users are unable to see the hidden category itself and are unable to see any subcategories or courses that are in the hidden category.

Moodle has a course and category management page to enable easily:

- creation of new courses and categories
- changing the order in which courses and categories appear on the page
- moving courses and categories into other categories
- editing, hiding, and deleting of courses and categories

You can access this page through the administration block via **Site administration** | **Courses** | **Manage courses and categories**:

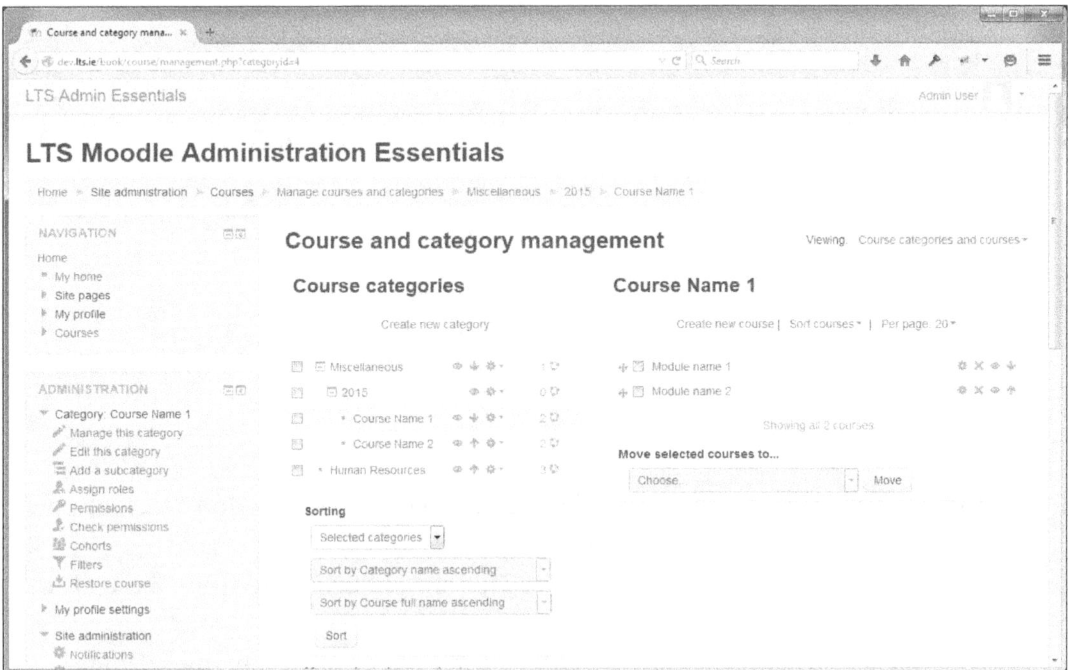

Course creation

To create a course in Moodle:

1. Log in as an administrator level, course creator, or manager user account.
2. Access the course management options in the **Administration** block by navigating to **Site administration** | **Courses** | **Manage courses and categories**.
3. Select the relevant category on the left where you want the course to be located, then click on the **Create new course** link on the right. This brings up the following page:

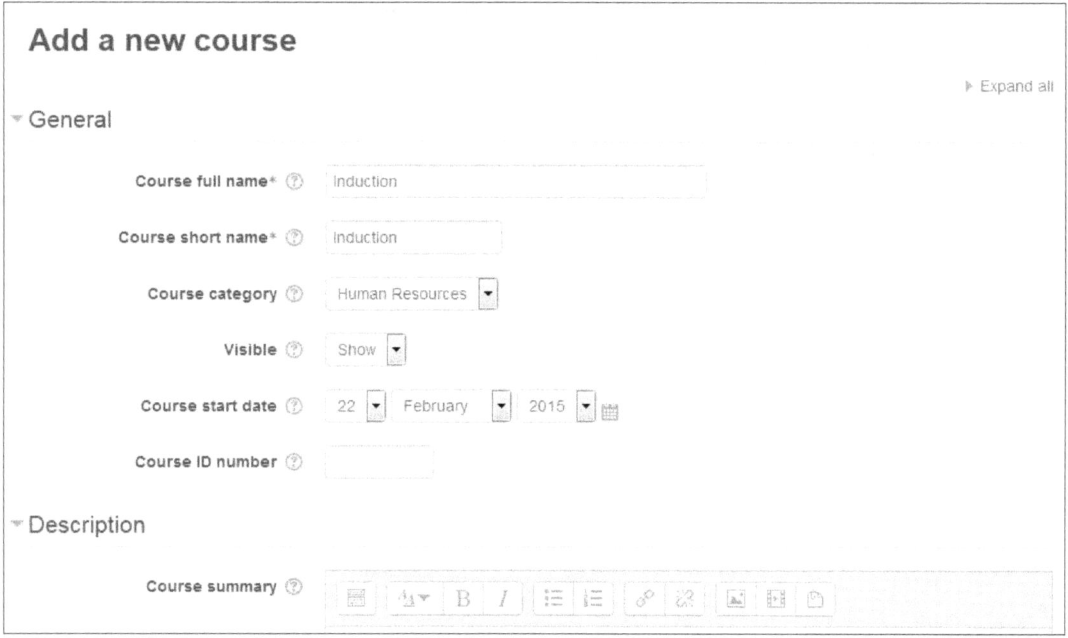

4. Alternatively, access the course listings page in the **Navigation** block under **Courses** and click on the **Add a new course** button.
5. Fill in the **Course full name** column. This should be a descriptive name for the course.
6. Fill in **Course short name**. This will be used for display in many settings, including navigation menu and breadcrumb links.
7. Select **Course start date** if relevant.
8. Enter **Course ID number** if required for identification purposes.

9. Enter a short description of the course in the **Course Summary** field. This is seen when users are browsing a category.
10. If you want to add an image that will appear in the course listing page, upload the image file into the **Course Summary files** field.
11. Under **Course Format,** change any of the default options if needed:
    - **Format** (we recommend for courses that are structured around sections or specific topics, that you select the **Topics Format**)
    - **Number of sections** (fill in your required number of areas to set out your course)
    - **Hidden Sections** (they are shown in collapsed form)
    - **Course Layout** (show all sections on one page)
12. Under **Appearance**, change any of the default options if needed:
    - **Force language** (English)
    - **News items to show** (set this to 0 if you want to disable the news forum)
    - **Show gradebook to students** (Yes)
    - **Show activity reports** (No)
13. Under **Files and uploads**, set the required **Maximum upload size** for your course. Set it as low as you expect it to be. However, this will impact the teacher and students uploading files to the course, forums, and assignments.
14. Under **Completion tracking**, set **Enable completion tracking** to **No** if you want to disable completion tracking. This must have already been enabled as a global site setting, but by default it is turned off.

[Completion tracking is used to determine whether an activity or resource has been completed by the student. This is configured on a per activity basis, such as a quiz being complete once a grade is received, or a forum activity is complete when two forum posts have been made by the user.]

15. Under **Guest access**, set **Allow guest access** to **Yes** if you want guests to access the course.
16. Under **Groups**, set **Group mode** to the required setting:
    - **No groups** (if you don't use groups in the course). This impacts the group mode for every activity in the course.
    - **Separate groups** (if you want to have groups isolated from each other).

- **Visible groups** (if you want to have groups, but not isolate them from each other).

17. Under **Groups**, set **Force group mode** as **YES** if you want every activity to have groups enabled.
18. If you want to rename your roles as they will appear in just this course (such as changing student to participant), change them under **Role renaming**.
19. Click on **Save changes** to save your course.

Uploading courses

An administrator can bulk create courses in Moodle using a spreadsheet, similar to how we uploaded users in the previous chapter. This can be created in Microsoft Excel, OpenOffice Calc, or a similar application like Google Docs. In this section, we will refer to Microsoft Excel.

The minimum information that is required, as data in the spreadsheet includes the shortname, fullname, and category.

Preparing the spreadsheet

To prepare your file for uploading courses:

1. Open Excel.
2. Create three column names in the first row seen here. These should be lowercase and no spaces:
   - shortname
   - fullname
   - category
3. Fill in the course details for shortname, fullname and category

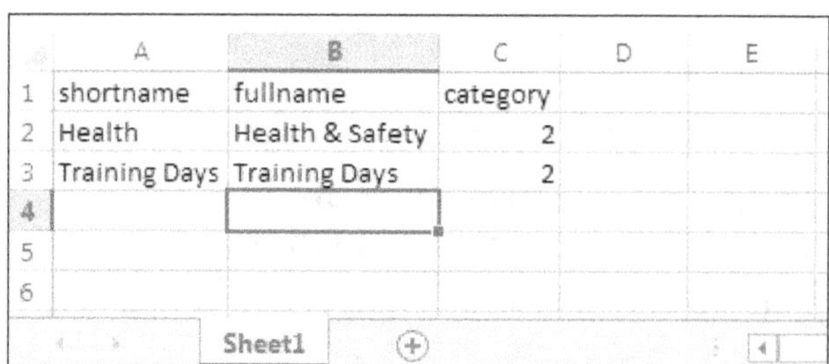

	A	B	C	D	E
1	shortname	fullname	category		
2	Health	Health & Safety	2		
3	Training Days	Training Days	2		
4					
5					
6					

Sheet1

4. For the category, this must be an existing category ID, with the default category miscellaneous having ID `1`. This is the number shown in the URL (`http://example.com/course/index.php?categoryid=3`). When viewing a category in this case, the category ID is `3`.
5. The Course upload `csv` file may also contain other fields which will allow additional configuration when creating the courses.
6. Repeat this process using a new row per course for all the courses that you want to create.
7. Under the File menu, select **Save As**.
8. Select `csv` (`Comma` delimited) (`*.csv`) for **Save as type**.
9. Click **Save** and Excel will give you a warning about the format.
10. Click **Yes** to continue to save the `csv` file.

Uploading the spreadsheet

On the Moodle site you can now proceed with uploading the spreadsheet.

1. Log in as an administrator user account.
2. Access the upload course options in the **Administration** block by navigating to **Site administration** | **Courses** | **Upload Courses**. This brings up the following page.

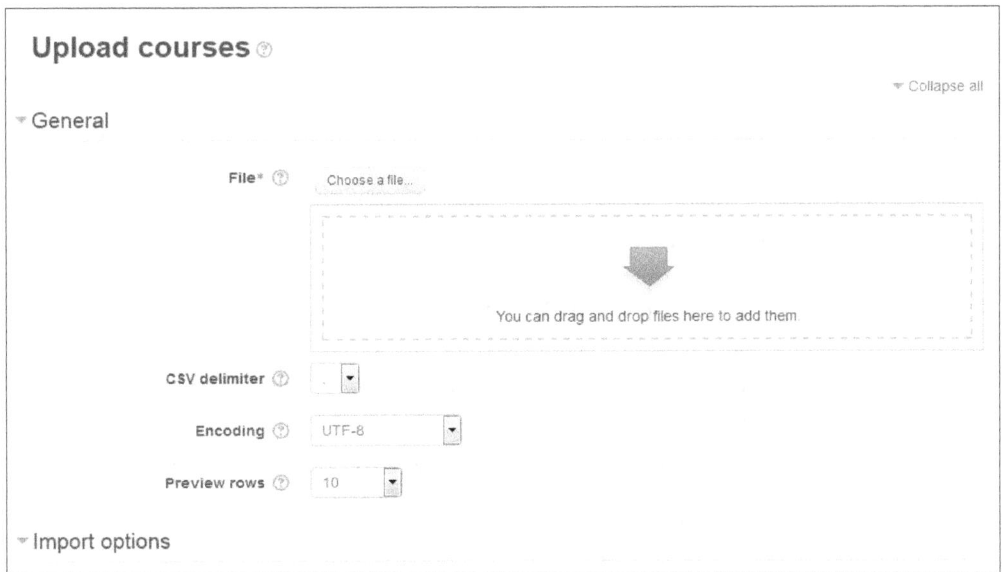

3. Click on **Choose a file...** to bring up the file picker.
4. Click on **Upload a file** and then click on **Browse**.
5. Find the file on your computer and then click on open to select it.
6. Click on **Upload this file.**
7. Change the **Preview** rows setting to a larger suitable number if you are uploading a lot of courses. This will enable you to preview that their details have been interpreted correctly.
8. Click on **Preview**. This will bring up the preview page before actually creating the courses.
9. Check the **Upload courses preview** of the courses is correct:

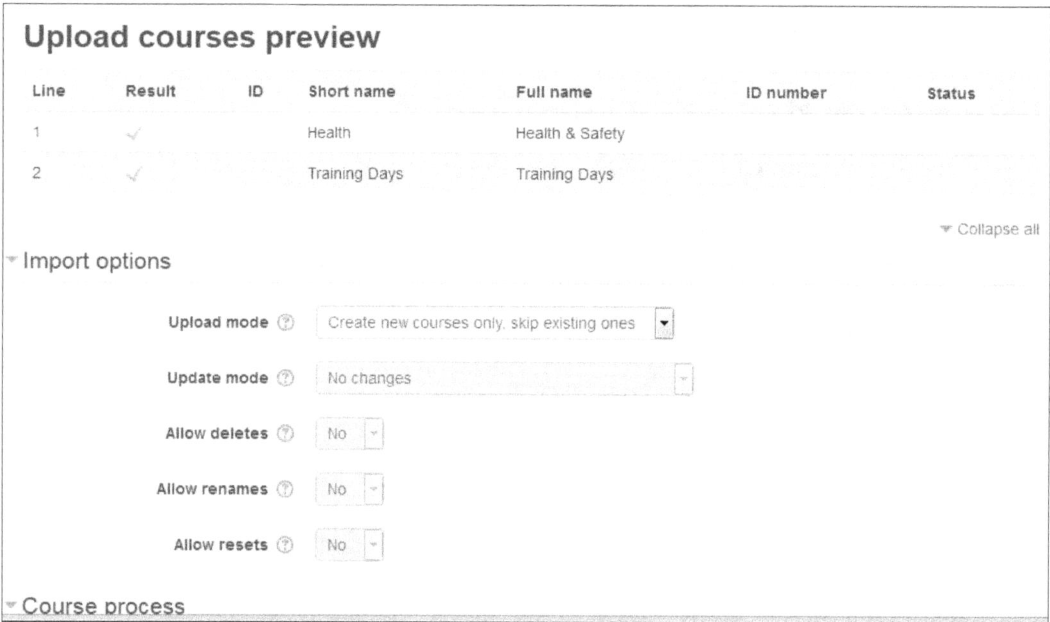

10. Under **Import options** | **Upload mode**, if you are creating new courses, select **Create new courses only, skip existing ones**.
    - Select **Only update existing courses** if you are updating existing courses.
    - Select **Create new courses, or update existing ones** if you are creating new courses and updating existing ones.

11. If updating courses, set **Update mode** to the required setting
    - **No changes** (disable all changes to existing courses)
    - **Update with CSV data only** (if you want to overwrite course data from the CSV file only)
    - **Update with CSV data and defaults** (if you want to overwrite course data both from the CSV file and form values)
    - **Fill in missing items from CSV data and defaults** (if you want to update the CSV file and form values for course data if not already specified)
12. If using a course template to populate the courses' content, select the relevant file for **Restore from this file after upload**. The course templates will be explained in more detail in the next section of this chapter.
13. If using an existing course to clone the courses' content, enter the relevant course shortname in the **Reset course after upload** field. Again, this will be explained in more detail later.
14. Under **Default course values**, these additional settings can be configured for any relevant fields that are not specified in the CSV file.

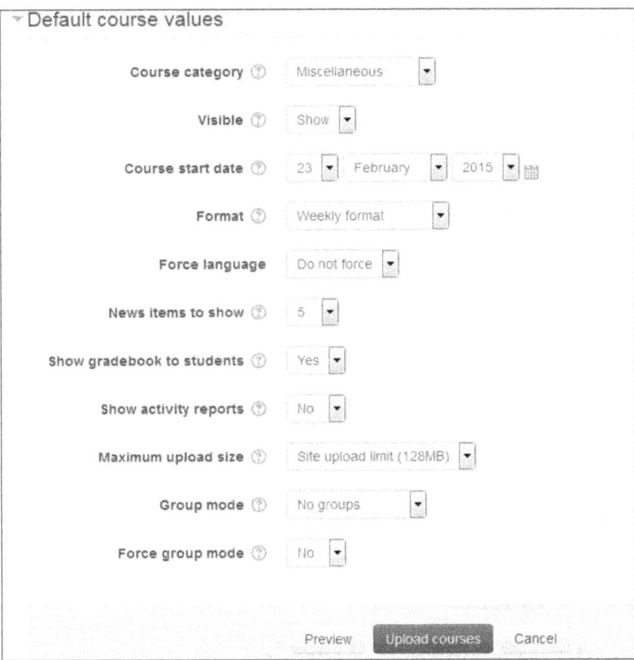

15. Click on the **Upload courses** button to save all changes.

Course templates

Course templates are useful for ensuring that courses are created to an agreed consistent or branded format and structure.

In Moodle 2.6 onward, there are a number of ways to implement this:

- Restore a previously backed up course `ZIP` file
- In **Upload courses**, as explained previously, you can specify an existing course to use as a template for the content of the courses, which are going to be created or updated

Here is an example of a sample template course and course section:

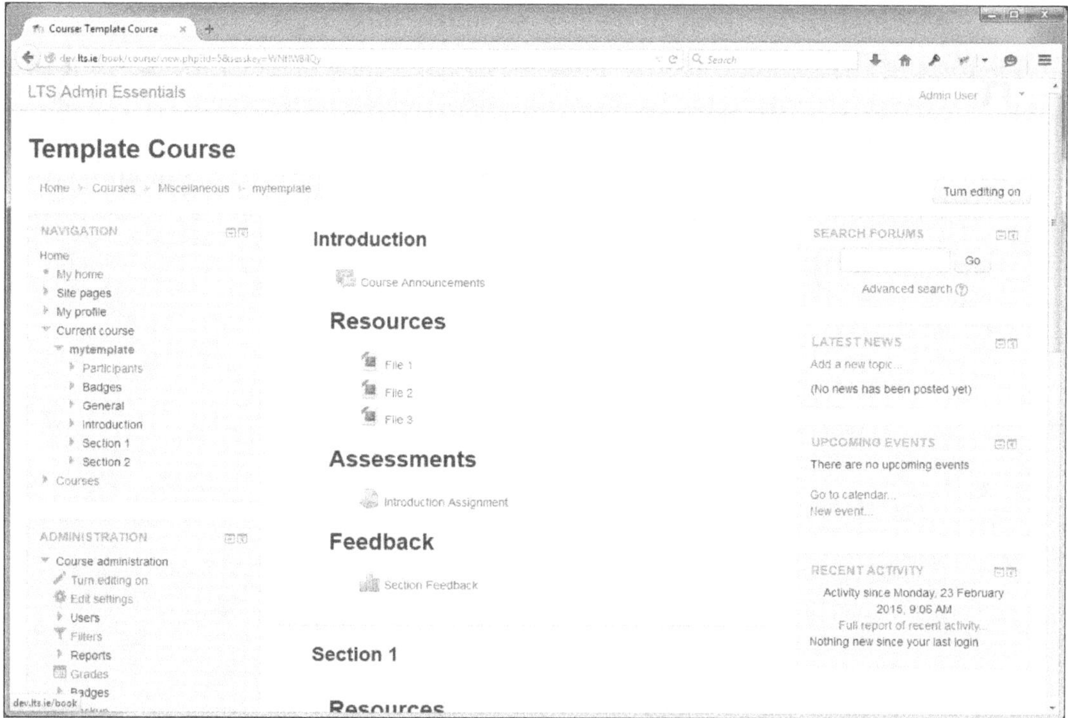

Restore a course

To restore a course in Moodle:

1. Log in as an administrator level user account.
2. Access the course management options in the **Administration** block by navigating to **Site administration** | **Courses** | **Restore course**.

3. From here, chose either of the following ways to begin the restoring process:
    1. Click on **Choose a file** to upload the backup file and click on **Restore** below the file upload area.
    2. Choose a file in the **Course backup area** or **User private backup area** and click on the **Restore** link to the right of the file.
4. Check that all content listed on the page is as expected, then click on **Continue**.
5. Depending on your account permissions, you can choose to restore the course as a new course or restore into an existing course.
6. To restore into a new course, choose the relevant category to add it, and then click on the **Continue** button in the **Restore as a new course** section.
7. To restore into the present course, choose whether to merge the backup into the course or to delete the current course contents that will overwrite it. Click on the **Continue** button in the **Restore into this course** section.
8. Select the activities, blocks, filters, and other items to be restored, and then click the **Next** button in the lower-right corner.
9. Change the **Course name**, **short name**, and **start date** values as necessary.
10. Review the list of items to be restored and deselect any items that should not be restored.
11. Click on **Next** to continue.

12. Check that everything is as required, otherwise click on the **Perform restore** button.
13. A progress bar will display once the restore is completed.
14. Click on the **Continue** button.

Clone a course

To clone a course in Moodle:

1. Log in as an administrator level, course creator, or manager user account.
2. Access the course management options in the **Administration** block by navigating to **Site administration | Courses | Upload courses**.
3. As before, click on **Choose a file** to bring up the file picker and continue to select the relevant courses upload `csv` file.
4. From here, there are three ways to specify the course that you want to use as the template course:
    1. Have an additional column in the `csv` upload file itself, called `templatecourse`, for each uploaded course. This should be the shortname of the existing course.
    2. In the **Restore from this file after upload** file picker field, select the relevant backup file.
    3. In the **Restore from this course after upload** field, enter the shortname of the existing course.

5. Click on **Upload courses** to save the changes.

Summary

In this chapter, we looked at the core administrator roles of course management in adding courses, adding categories for course organization, and bulk uploading courses. We also looked at ways to duplicate an existing course as a template for new courses.

In the next chapter, we focus on the management of the Moodle site appearance, and how it can be customized to portray a branded version of Moodle.

Managing Site Appearance

In the previous chapter, we looked at how to deal with course management by adding courses, adding categories for course organization, and bulk uploading courses. We also looked at ways to duplicate an existing course as a template for new courses.

In this chapter, we will be examining ways in which we can enhance the appearance of your Moodle site, extending it beyond the default setup.

We will also deal with the essential areas of the site appearance that every administrator might have to deal with:

- Configuring the landing page
- Configuring the front page
- Configuring global theme settings
- Configuring the default Clean theme
- Configuring the default More theme
- Cloning an existing theme to create and extend a new theme

Configuring the landing page

Configuring the landing page allows you to control what a visitor will have access to see on your Moodle site before they have logged in.

The default configuration allows a visitor who's not yet logged in to see your main front page. Depending on what you have configured to display on your front page, as discussed in the next section, *Configuring the front page*, they can potentially see your course list, with their summaries, your news items, and any other announcement information you may have put there for your users.

If you want to prevent your front page from being viewed by anyone from the internet, you can force all the users to the login page as their initial landing page. This forces users to log in validly to your Moodle site before they can view any further pages. You can also make an appealing visual feature out of your login page, by adding relevant inspiring background images or increase its effectiveness for referrals by including useful contact information.

To configure the landing page setting, to enforce user logins, perform the following:

1. Go to the **Administration** block by navigating to **Site administration** | **Security** | **Site policies**:

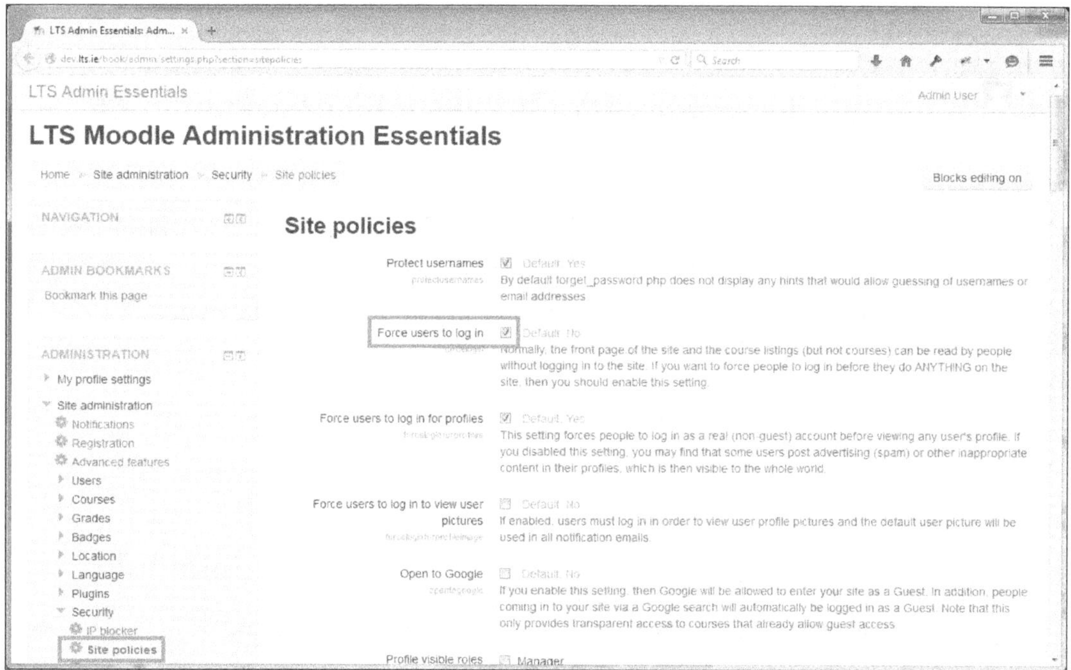

2. Tick the **Force users to log in** option to enable the site to redirect all non logged in users to the login page, instead of the front page.
3. Click on **Save** changes.

Configuring the front page

This is the initial page, which a visitor will see on your Moodle site after logging in. If the user has not yet logged in, your visitor's initial landing page will be either the front page or the login page, depending on your configuration.

Hence, it's essential to make it user friendly, engaging the learner and making their task easier to accomplish, whether it's finding their next work due, or connecting with other users.

The front page can be easily customized by adding activities, resources, and blocks, similar to course pages.

To configure the front page settings, go to the **Administration** block by navigating to **Site administration | Front page | Front page settings**. The following options are available under **Front page settings**:

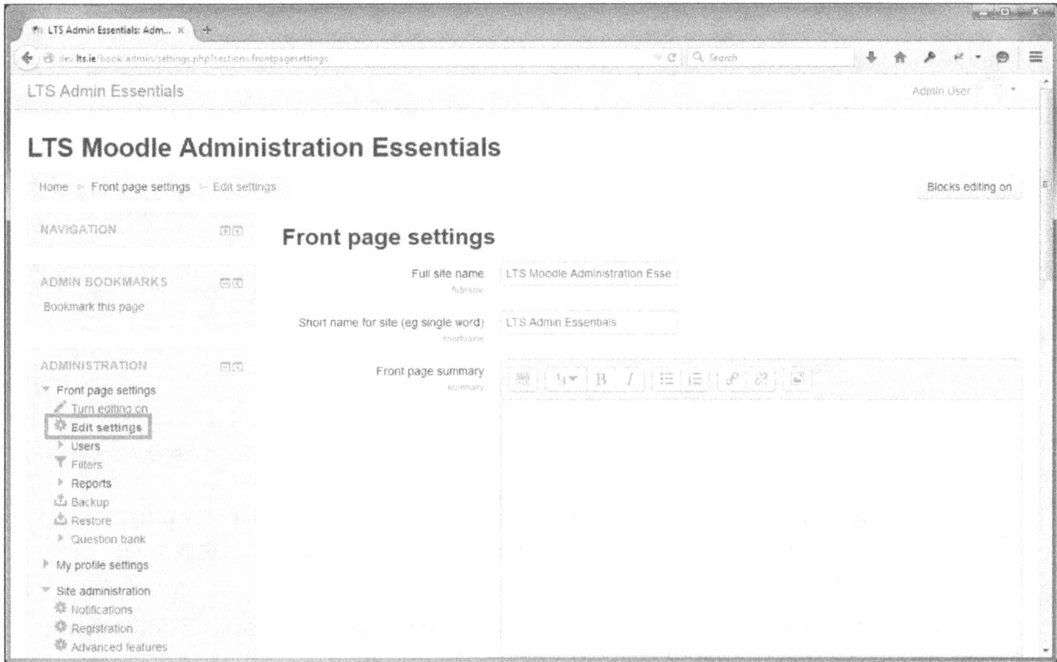

- **Full site name**: This appears at the top of each page.
- **Short name for site**: This appears at the top of each page and in the browser title and many other places, so choose a short name that people will understand.
- **Front page summary**: This summary will appear on the front page and may contain text, images, and other HTML features.

- **Front page**: This allows you to set predefined content displayed in the main section of the front page and their ordering. You can select multiple items from the following options: **News items, List of courses, List of categories, Combo list** (of both courses and categories), and **Course search box.**

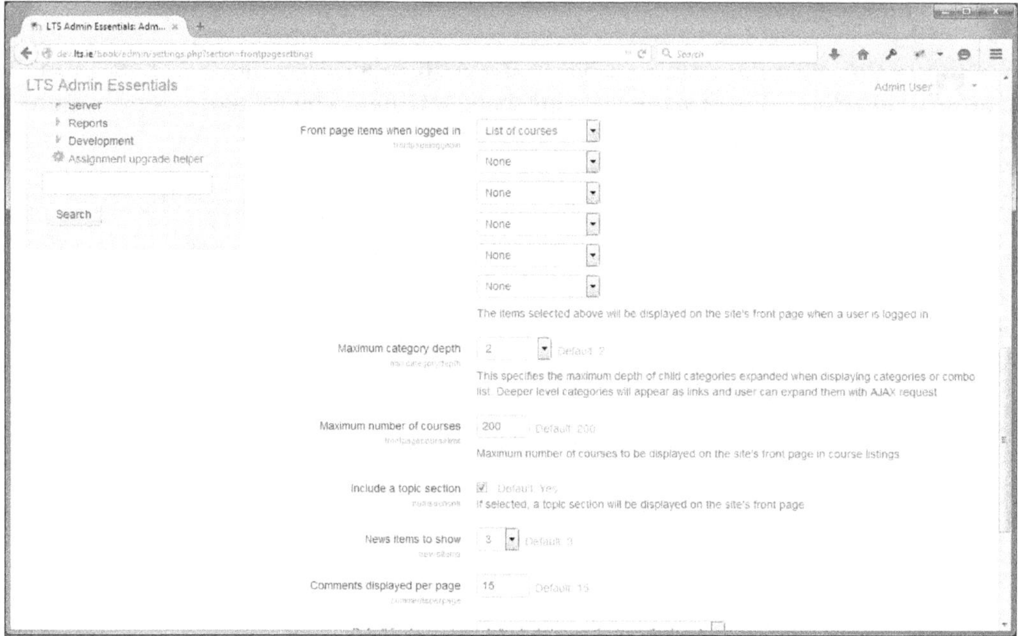

- **Front page items when logged in**: This allows you to set the content displayed in the main section of the front page, and its ordering once the user is logged in.
- **Maximum category depth**: This refers to the course category structure of the site and sets the level for child category expansion so that you can see categories and subcategories.
- **Maximum number of courses**: This sets the maximum number of courses that can be displayed under the course listings.
- **Include a topic section**: This enables a topic section to display on the front page, which allows you to add activities and resources as required. It is a common practice to use this area to have landing page content, such as a welcome message or an image of the organization.
- **News items to show**: This limits the number of items to show in the news section if selected in the items to display.
- **Comments displayed per page**: This limits the number of comments displayed within a comments block, if enabled.

- **Default frontpage role**: This should be set to the default authenticated user on front page option, as this allows any logged in user to participate in any activities included on the front page. It can also be set to student.
- **Save changes**: This will save any of the changes to the front page so that you can see how they look.

Global theme settings

The global theme settings page allows you to customize a great deal of highly visible sections of your Moodle site.

The global theme settings page includes the custom menu in the main navigation banner that is commonly referred to as the top navigation menu, which is normally at the top of each page, but can be placed at the bottom of each page.

This also includes the user profile menu that along with the custom menu, allows you to extend the user navigation experience with whichever additional or heavily used resources they will need easy access to.

The global theme settings page also includes the option of allowing different themes to be chosen for different circumstances, such as per course or per user.

To configure the general theme settings, go to the **Administration** block by navigating to **Site administration** | **Appearance** | **Themes** | **Theme settings**, and this brings up the **Theme settings** page:

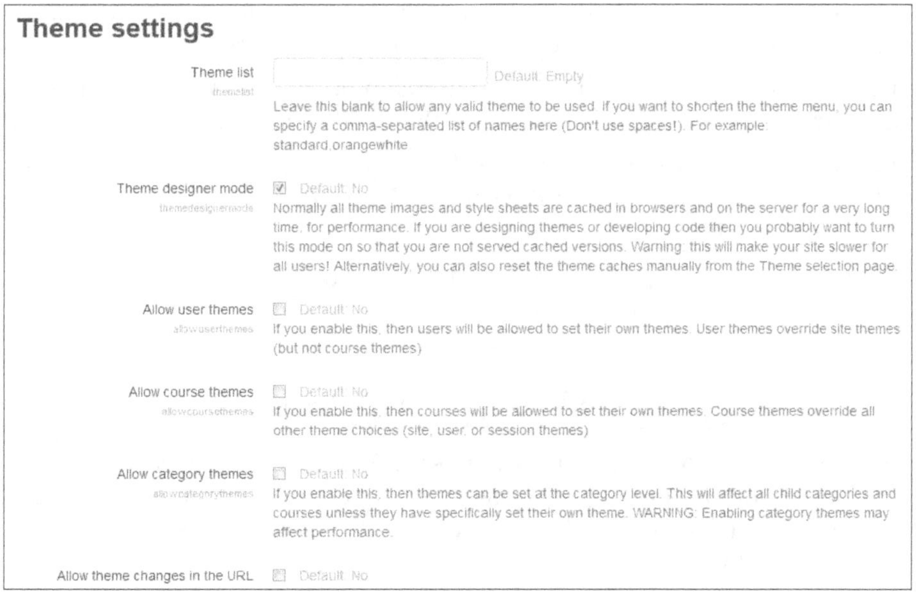

- **Theme list**: If you are allowing users or courses to select a specific theme, you can limit that choice by including the themes' short names in a comma-separated list here.
- **Theme designer mode**: This turns off all theme caching, so it is useful for testing the design and progress of a new theme. Please note that this will make your site slower to all users.
- **Allow user themes**: This allows users to choose their own theme from the theme menu, overriding site themes, but not course themes.
- **Allow course themes**: This allows themes to be set per course, overriding all other theme settings.
- **Allow category themes**: This allows themes to be set per category. Please note that this may make your site slower to all users.
- **Allow theme changes in the URL**: This is useful for debugging potential theme issues by comparison with other theme performance. This allows the theme to be specified by its short name at the end of the URL by adding the theme—`themeshortname`.
- **Allow users to hide blocks**: This allows users to hide or show blocks in their view only.
- **Allow blocks to use the dock**: This allows users to move blocks to and from a special dock section. **Docking** is a feature in Moodle where the user can elect to move a block from the main page off to the left side of the screen to save space. It will then show the name of the block on the side of the screen, and expand when it is clicked on.
- **Custom menu items**: This allows link items to be added to the custom menu for permanent navigation access across all main pages.
- **User menu items**: This allows link items to be added to the user menu, which appears across all main pages under the user's profile name and image.
- **Enable device detection**: This enables device detection, such as mobile phones and tablets, to assist the user with specific theme and other features selection.
- **Device detection regular expressions**: This enables more granular device detection by phrase recognition.

Introducing the Clean theme

The **Clean** theme is one of the default themes for Moodle 2.8. It is based on the well-known Bootstrap theme, which was originally created for Moodle version 2.5, by Bas Brands, David Scotson, and Mary Evans with the help of Stuart Lamour, Mark Aberdour, and Paul Hibbitts.

The **Clean** theme includes the main Bootstrap framework features for supporting a responsive, modular, and mobile-first web site. This ensures that the layout of web pages adjusts dynamically, based on the characteristics of the device used to view the web pages, be it desktop, tablet, or mobile phone.

The **Clean** theme is characterized by a clean, minimalist, and uncluttered layout with a sparing use of color.

Configuring the Clean theme

To configure the Clean theme, perform the following:

1. In the **Administration** block, navigate to **Site administration** | **Appearance** | **Themes** | **Clean**:

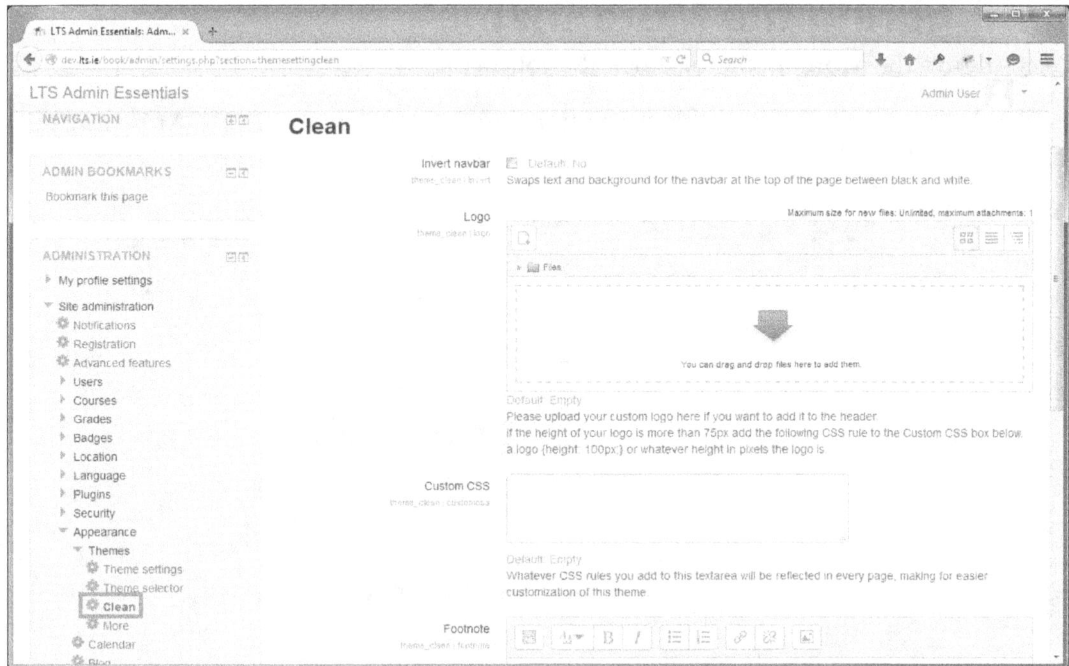

2. Tick the **Invert navbar** option to swap colors if preferred.
3. For the **Logo**, upload your own logo using the file picker.
4. If your uploaded logo is more than 75px in height, add the following to the **Custom CSS** column:

```
a.logo {height: XXXpx;}
```

5. You can also add some HTML as a footnote to each page as **Footnote**.
6. Click on **Save changes** if you changed any options and want to save the new values.

Introducing the More theme

The **More** theme is the second of the default themes for Moodle 2.8. More is a theme that allows you as an administrator to easily customize your Moodle site's look and feel, directly from the web interface.

The More theme is characterized by a responsive, minimalist, and uncluttered layout with a flexible use of color depending on the settings.

Configuring the More theme

To configure the **More** theme perform the following:

1. In the **Administration** block, navigate to **Site administration** | **Appearance** | **Themes** | **More**:

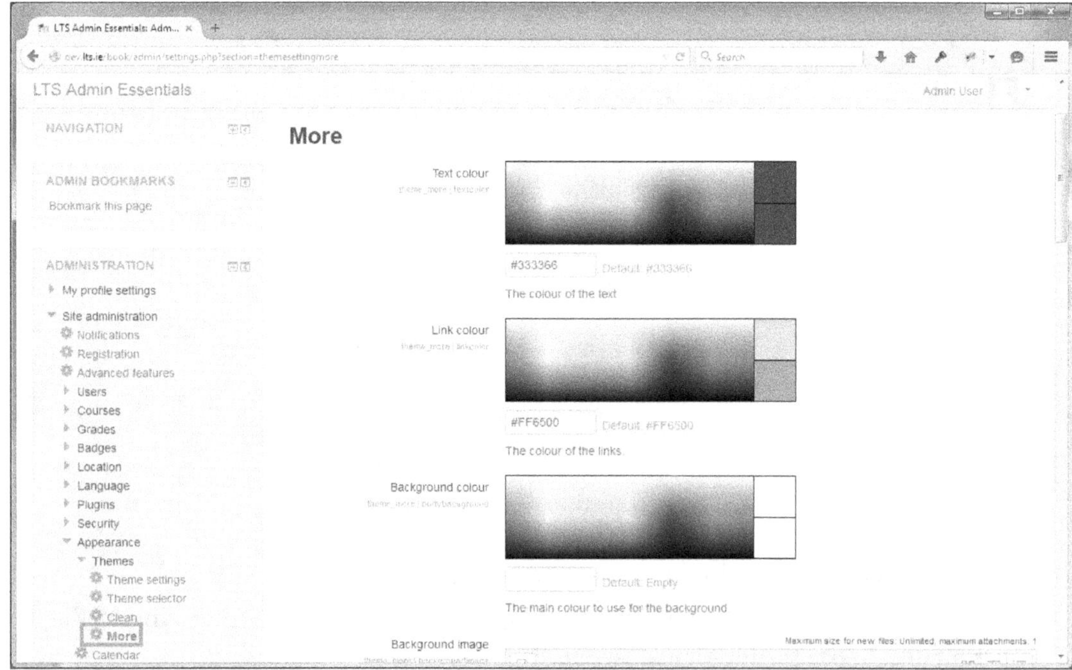

2. To change the **Text colour**, **Link colour**, or **Background colour**, use the relevant color picker, or directly type in the RGB hex value. Note that you can even specify transparency values such as rgba(255,255,255,0.8).
3. To configure **Background image**, upload the relevant image file with the file picker.
4. The background image can also be set to a specific repeat pattern with **Background repeat**.
5. The background image can further be set to position itself using **Background position**.
6. The background image can finally be set to fix itself using **Background fixed**:

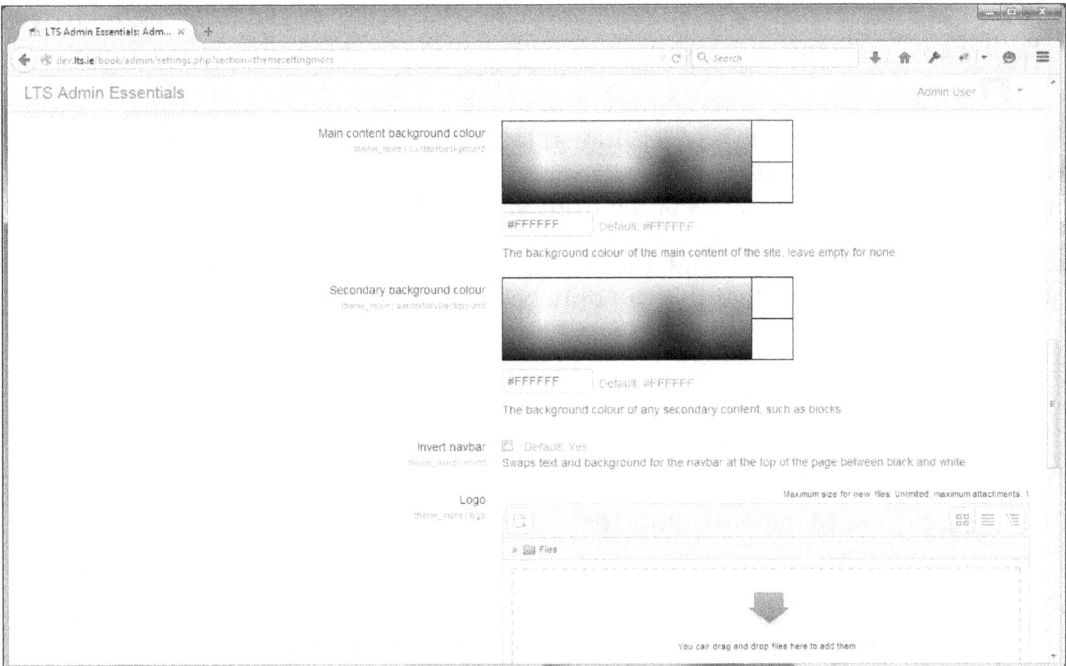

7. To change **Main content background colour**, which is the main page background, use the relevant color picker, or directly type in the RGB hex value.
8. To change **Secondary background colour**, which is used for blocks and other secondary content, use the relevant color picker or directly type in the RGB hex value.
9. Tick the **Invert navbar** option to swap colors if required.

10. For the **Logo**, upload your own logo using the file picker.
11. If your uploaded logo is more than 75px in height, add the following to **Custom CSS**:

    ```
    a.logo {height: XXXpx;}
    ```

12. You can also add some HTML as a footnote to each page as the **Footnote**(footer throughout your Moodle site).
13. Click on **Save changes**.

Cloning a theme

If you would like to make a theme custom change, which is unavailable with the two default themes, **Clean** and **More**, you have the option to clone one of the themes and extend its code further in the implementation of your appearance requirements.

For instance, if you want to add additional JavaScript or JScript to include more interactivity for the learners for a specific section of the site, or if you want to have more control over the elements of the front page and what it contains.

Here, we are going to go through the steps of cloning the **Clean** theme and then customize it. Please note that this can only be done on the server folder, which contains the Moodle site, and can't be implemented via the Moodle interface itself.

To clone the **Clean** theme perform the following:

1. Access your Moodle server with the appropriate permissions to create folders and files.
2. Go to your Moodle site directory, and then go to the **theme** directory.
3. Create a fully recursive copy of the `clean` folder and rename it `cleantheme` or whichever new name you wish.
4. Go into the `cleantheme` directory and view the subfolder and files contained there as follows:

```
config.php  lang  layout  lib.php  pix  README.txt  settings.php  style  version.php
```

    - `config.php`: This file contains the theme configurations, some of which will need renaming later.
    - `lib.php`: This file contains the theme functions, some of which will need renaming.
    - `settings.php`: This file contains the theme settings, some of which will need renaming.

- `version.php`: This file contains the theme version number and plugin component details, some of which will need renaming.
- `/lang/`: This folder contains all included language subdirectories deemed essential for your Moodle site.
- `/lang/en/`: This folder contains the default en, or English language files.
- `/lang/en/theme_clean.php`: Importantly, this file needs to be renamed to `theme_cleantheme.php` (or whichever new name you use). This file contains the theme language strings, some of which will need renaming.
- `/layout/`: This folder contains the layout files for the theme, which control display aspects for the Moodle pages.
- `/layout/columns1.php`: This file contains the theme layout file for pages with a one column layout, for example, content only.
- `/layout/columns2.php`: This file contains the theme layout file for pages with a two column layout, for example, one side and content.
- `/layout/columns3.php`: This file contains the theme layout file for pages with a three column layout, for example, two sides and central content.
- `/layout/embedded.php`: This file contains the theme layout file for pages with embedded content, for example, iframes.
- `/layout/maintenance.php`: This file contains the theme layout file for maintenance pages with no blocks, links or API calls which would trigger database or cache retrieval.
- `/layout/secure.php`: This file contains the theme layout file for secure pages, for example, safebrowser or securewindow.
- `/style/`: This folder contains the CSS files for the theme.
- `/style/custom.css`: This file contains all the CSS for the theme.
- `/pix/`: This folder contains all the images used in the theme, including a screenshot of one of the full theme pages, to use in the Theme selector Change theme process, thus giving a preview of how the theme will look when selected.

5. For all of the files specified earlier, they need to be searched, and each instance of the word clean needs to be replaced with `cleantheme` or whichever new name you have chosen.
6. Also remember to rename the file called `theme_clean.php` in the `/lang/en` folder to `theme_cleantheme.php`, or whichever new name you have chosen.

7. You now need to install the new theme. This may automatically start if you refresh the browser while logged in. Otherwise, go to **Administration | Notifications** to start the theme installation process:

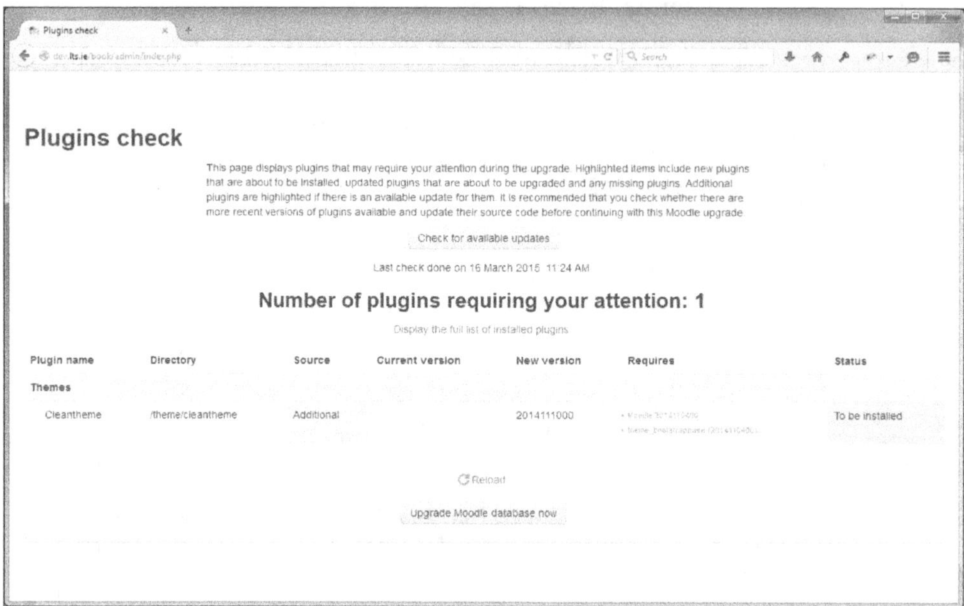

8. Click on **Upgrade Moodle database now** to complete the new theme installation.
9. Once your new theme is installed, you can set it as the default theme as shown in the following steps:

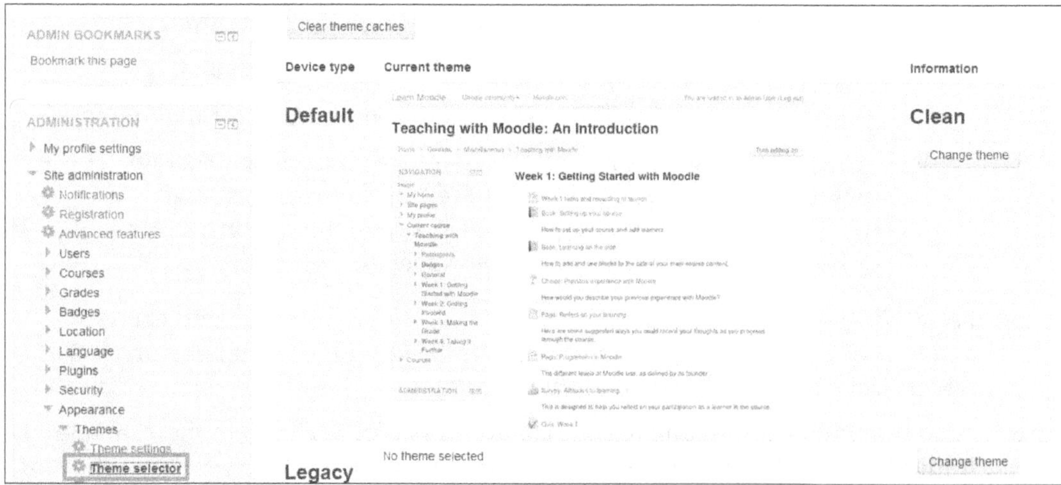

1. Navigate to **Administration** | **Appearance** | **Themes** | **Theme selector** to start.
2. Click on the **Change** theme for the relevant device. The default device theme covers all devices, unless the mobile or tablet device themes are already specified.
3. Locate your new theme, `cleantheme`, with its preview screenshot and click on the **Use theme** button to its right.

When using a theme like Clean or More or one based on them, you do not need to create a mobile or tablet-specific theme as these are bootstrap-based themes, which are responsive in nature and work well on mobile and tablet devices.

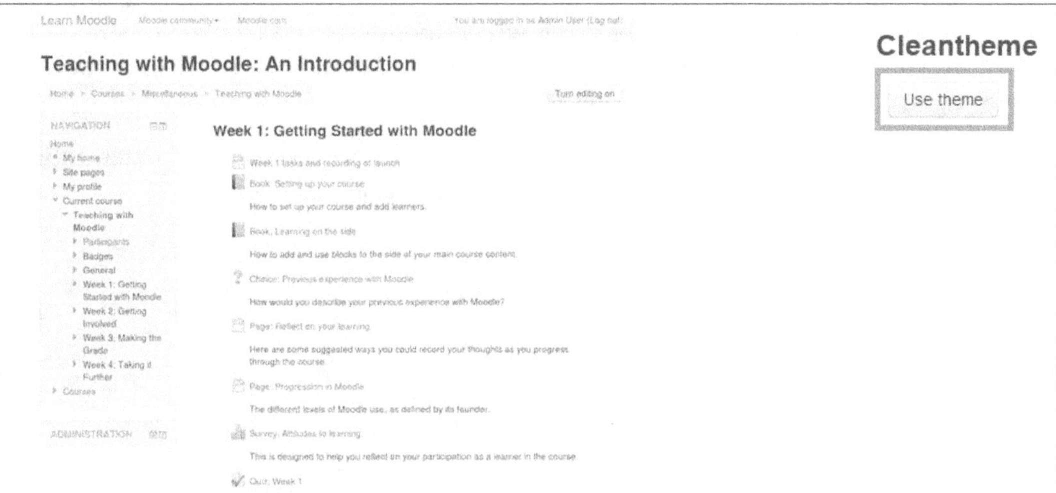

4. Click on **Continue**.
5. Click on the **Clear** theme caches to ensure that all the new theme settings, configurations, and CSS are being cached and displayed correctly.
6. Your new theme should now display.

10. You can now begin to modify the new theme files directly in their server folder as required. This avoids affecting the default original themes in any way, and keeps them intact for further cloning if and when required.
11. Alternatively, you can follow from step 7 onwards if you have had a new theme designed for you and have uploaded it to the theme folder, or if you have decided to use one of the freely available themes in the Moodle plugins database at `https://moodle.org/plugins/index.php`.

Summary

In this chapter, we focused on the management of the Moodle site's appearance and how it can be customized to portray a branded and focused version of Moodle.

We looked at the different methods of implementing this, from the available options for customizing the front page, to selecting which theme should be used where, and by who, adding to the available theme options, and how to extend the default themes, by uploading your branded logo for instance.

In the next chapter, we will be examining ways in which to enhance and extend the permissions of the users, by means of managing their role permissions.

5
Role Management

In the previous chapter, we looked at how to enhance the appearance of your Moodle site, extending it beyond the default setup. In this chapter, we will be examining ways in which to enhance and extend the permissions of the users, so that they can do something extra beyond their default capabilities, by means of managing their role permissions.

Roles play a key part in the ability of the Moodle site. They are able to restrict the access of users to only the data they should have access to, and whether or not they are able to alter it or add to it. In each course, every user will have been assigned a role when they are enrolled, such as teacher, student, or customized role.

In this chapter, we deal with the essential areas of role management that every administrator may have to deal with:

- Cloning a role
- Creating a new role
- Creating a course requester role
- Overriding a permission in a role in a course
- Testing a role
- Manually adding a role to a user in a course
- Enabling self-enrolment for a course

Understanding terminologies

There are some key terms used to describe users' abilities in Moodle and how they are defined, which are as follows:

- **Role**: A role is a set or collection of permissions on different capabilities. There are default roles like teacher and student, which have predefined sets of permissions.
- **Capability**: A capability is a specific behavior in Moodle, such as Start new discussions (`mod/forum:startdiscussion`), which can have a permission set within a role such as **Allow** or **Not set/Inherit**:

- **Permission**: Permission is associated with a capability. There are four possible values: allow, prevent, prohibit, or not set.
    - **Not set**: This means that that there is not a specific setting for this user role, and Moodle will determine if it is allowed, if set in a higher context.
    - **Allow**: The permission is explicitly granted for the capability.
    - **Prevent**: The permission is removed for the capability, even if allowed in a higher context. However, it can be overridden at a specific context.
    - **Prohibit**: The permission is completely denied and cannot be overridden at any lower context.

By default, the only configuration option displayed is **Allow**. To show the full list of options in the role edit page, click on the **Show advanced** button, just above the **Filter** option, as shown in the following image.

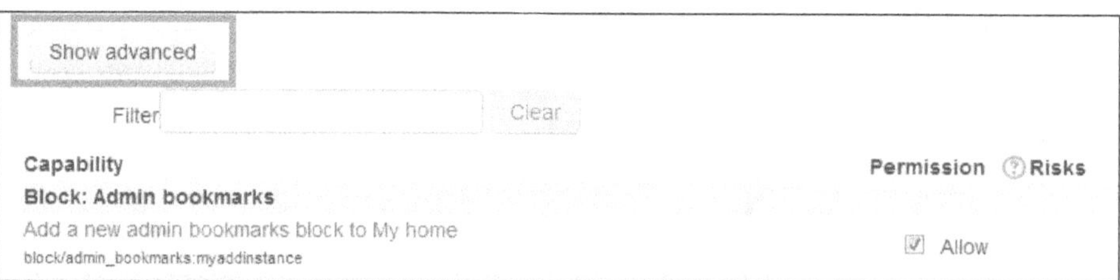

- **Context**: A context is an area of Moodle, such as the whole system, a category, a course, an activity, a block, or a user. A role will have permission for a capability on a specific context.

An example of this will be where a student can start a discussion in a specific forum. This is set up by enabling a permission to **Allow** for the capability **Start new discussions** for a **Student** role on that specific forum.

Standard roles

There are a number of different roles configured in Moodle, by default these are:

- **Site administrator**: The site administrator can do everything on the site including creating the site structure, courses, activities, and resources, and managing user accounts.
- **Manager**: The manager can access courses and modify them. They usually do not participate in teaching courses.
- **Course creator**: The course creator can create courses when assigned rights in a category.
- **Teacher**: The teacher can do anything within a course, including adding and removing resources and activities, communicating with students, and grading them.
- **Non-editing teacher**: The non-editing teacher can teach and communicate in courses and grade students, but cannot alter or add activities, nor change the course layout or settings.
- **Student**: The student can access and participate in courses, but cannot create or edit resources or activities within a course.
- **Guest**: The guest can view courses if allowed, but cannot participate. Guests have minimal privileges, and usually cannot enter text anywhere.
- **Authenticated user**: The role all logged in users get.
- **Authenticated user on the front page role**: A logged in user role for the front page only.

Managing role permissions

Let's learn how to manage permissions for existing roles in Moodle.

Cloning a role

It is possible to duplicate an existing role in Moodle. The main reasons for doing this will be so that you can have a variation of the existing role, such as a teacher, but with the role having reduced capabilities. For instance, to stop a teacher being able to add or remove students to the course, this process will be achieved by creating a course editing role, which is a clone of the standard `editingteacher` role with enrolment aspects removed. This is typically done when students are added to courses centrally with a student management system.

To duplicate a role, in this case editing teacher:

1. Log in as an administrator level user account.
2. In the **Administration** block, navigate to **Site administration** | **Users** | **Permissions** | **Define roles**:

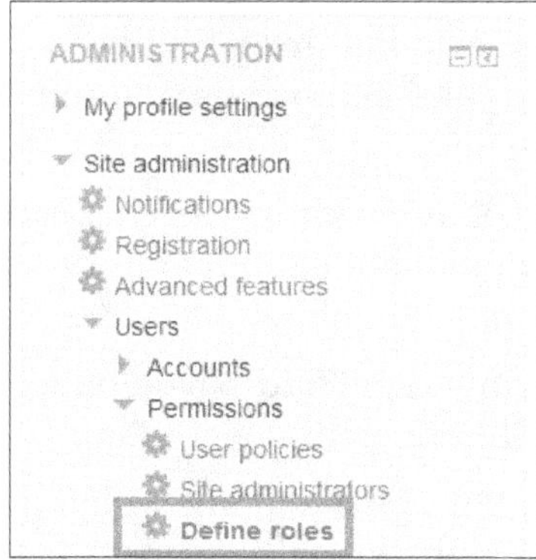

3. Click on the **Add a new role** button:

4. Select an existing role from the **Use role or archetype** dropdown.
5. Click on **Continue**:

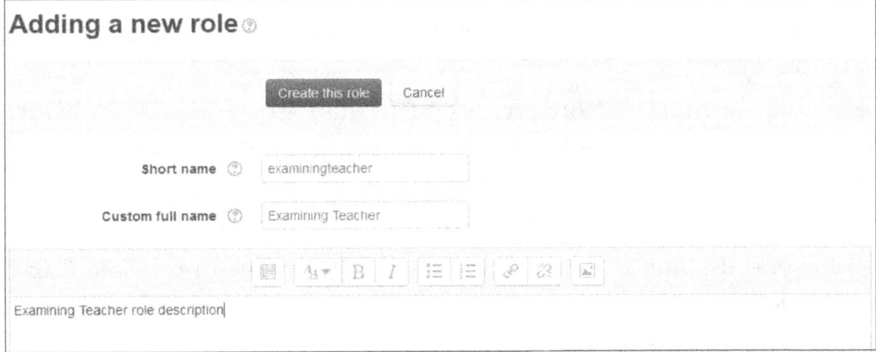

6. Enter the short role name in the **Short name** field. This must be unique.
7. Enter the full role name in the **Custom full name** field. This is what appears on the user interface in Moodle.
8. Enter an explanation for the role in the **Description** field. This should explain why the role was created, and what changes from default were planned.
9. Scroll to the bottom of the page.
10. Click on **Create this role**.

This will create a duplicate version of the teacher role with all the same permissions and capabilities.

Creating a new role

It is also possible to create a new role. The main reason for doing this would be to have a specific role to do a specific task and nothing else, such as a user that can manage users only. This is the alternative to cloning one of the existing roles, and then disabling everything except the one set of capabilities required.

To create a new role:

1. Log in as an administrator level user account.
2. In the **Administration** block, navigate to **Site administration** | **Users** | **Permissions** | **Define roles**.
3. Click on the **Add a new role** button.
4. Select `No role` from the **Use role or archetype** dropdown.
5. Click on **Continue**.
6. Enter the short role name in the **Short name** field. This must be unique.
7. Enter the full role name in the **Custom full name** field. This is what appears on the user interface in Moodle.
8. Enter an explanation for the role in the **Description** field. This should explain why the role was created.
9. Select the appropriate **Role archetype**, in this case, **None**. The role archetype determines the permissions when a role is reset to default and any new permissions for the role when the site is upgraded.
10. Select **Context types where this role may be assigned**.
11. Set the permissions as required by searching for the appropriate **Capability** and clicking on **Allow**.
12. Scroll to the bottom of the page.
13. Click on **Create this role**.

This will create the new role with the settings as defined.

If you want the new role to appear in the course listing, you must enable it by navigating to **Administration** block | **Site administration** | **Appearance** | **Courses** | **Course Contacts**.

Creating a course requester role

There is a core Moodle feature that enables users to request a course to be created. This is not normally used, especially as students and most teachers just have responsibility within their own course context. So, it can be useful to create a role just with this ability, so that a faculty or department administrator can request a new course space when needed, without giving the ability to all users.

There are a few steps in this process:

1. Remove the capability from other roles.
2. Set up the new role.
3. Assign the role to a user at the correct context.
4. Firstly, we remove the capability from other roles by altering the authenticated user role as shown:
    1. In the **Administration** block, navigate to **Site administration** | **Users** | **Permissions** | **Define roles**.
    2. Click on edit for the **Authenticated user** role:

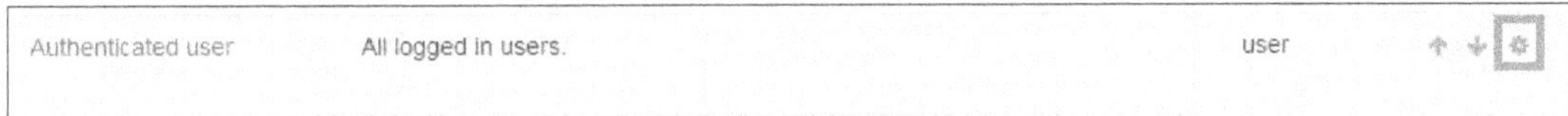

    3. Enter the `request` text into **Filter**.
    4. Select the **Not set** radio button under `moodle/course:request` to change the **Allow** permission.

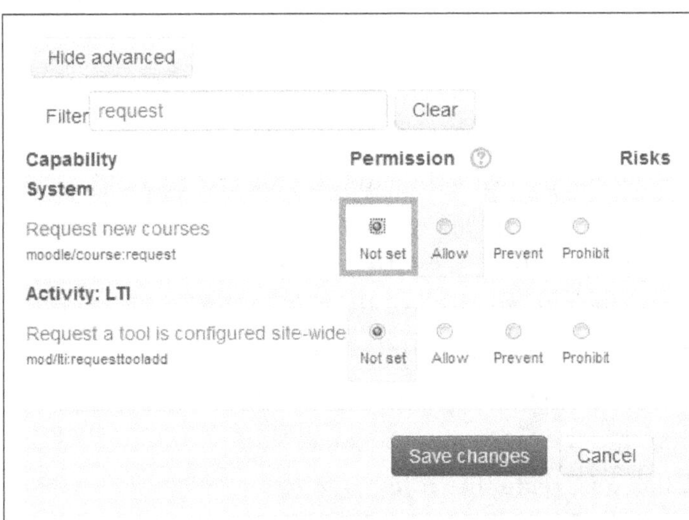

5. Scroll to the bottom of the page.
6. Click on **Save changes**.

5. Next, we create the new role with the specific capability set to **Allow**.
   7. In the **Administration** block, navigate to **Site administration | Users | Permissions | Define roles**.
   8. Click on the **Add a new role** button.
   9. Select **No role** from the **Use role or archetype** dropdown.
   10. Click on **Continue**.

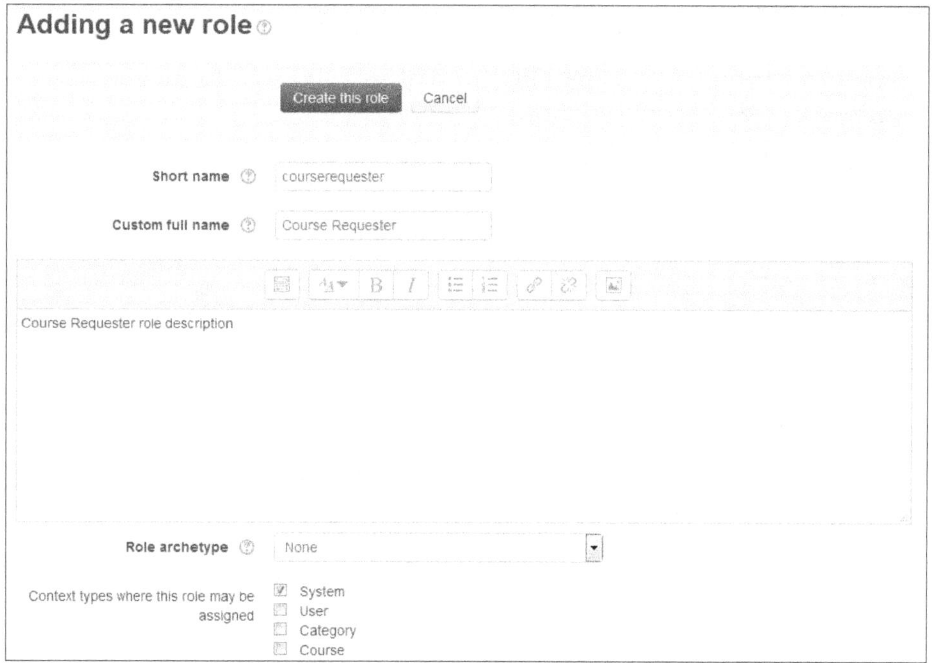

11. Enter `courserequester` in the **Short name** field.
12. Enter `Course Requester` in the **Custom full name** field. This is what appears on the user interface in Moodle.
13. Enter the explanation for the role in the **Description** field.
14. Select system under **Context types where this role may be assigned**.
15. Change `moodle/course:request` to **Allow**.
16. Scroll to the bottom of the page.
17. Click on **Create this role**.

6. Lastly, you assign the role to a user at system level. This is different from giving a role to a user in a course.
    1. In the **Administration** block, navigate to **Site administration** | **Users** | **Permissions** | **Assign system roles**.

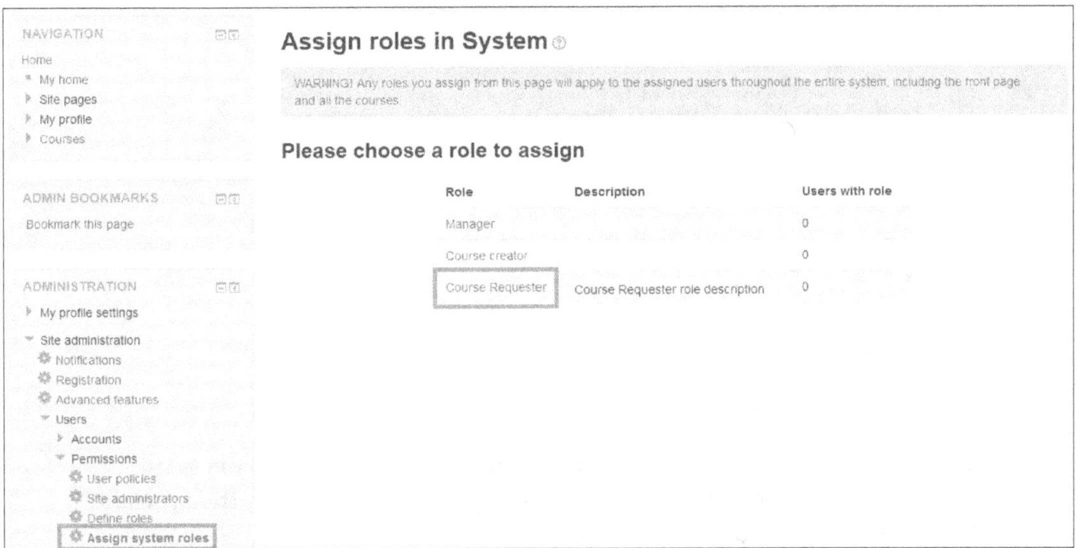

    2. Click on **Course Requester**.
    3. Search for the specific user in the **Potential user list**.
    4. Select the user from the list, using the **Search** filter if required.
    5. Click on the **Add** button.

Any roles you assign from this page will apply to the assigned users throughout the entire system, including the front page and all the courses.

Applying a role override for a specific context

You can change how a specific role behaves in a certain context by enabling an override, thereby granting or removing, the permission in that context.

An example of this is, in general, students cannot rate a forum post in a forum in their course. When ratings are enabled, only the manager, teacher, and non-editing teacher roles are those with permission to rate the posts. So, to enable the students to rate posts, you need to change the permissions for the student role on that specific forum.

Browse to the forum where you want to allow students to rate forum posts. This process assumes that the rating has been already enabled in the forum.

1. From the **Forum** page, go to the **Administration** block, then to **Forum administration**, and click on the link to **Permissions**.

2. Scroll down the page to locate the permission **Rate posts**. This is the `mod/forum:rate` capability. By default, you should not see the student role listed to the right of the permission.

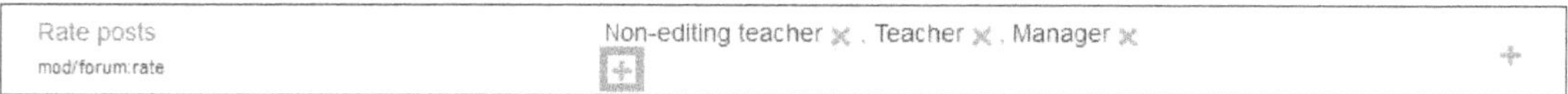

3. Click on the plus sign (+) that appears below the roles already listed for the **Rate posts** permission.
4. Select **Student** from the **Select role** menu, and click on the **Allow** button. **Student** should now appear in the list next to the **Rate posts** permission.

Participants will now be able to rate each other's posts in this forum. Making the change in this forum does not impact other forums.

Testing a role

It is possible to use the **Switch role to** feature to see what the other role behaves like in the different contexts. However, the best way to test a role is to create a new user account, and then assign that user the role in the correct context as follows:

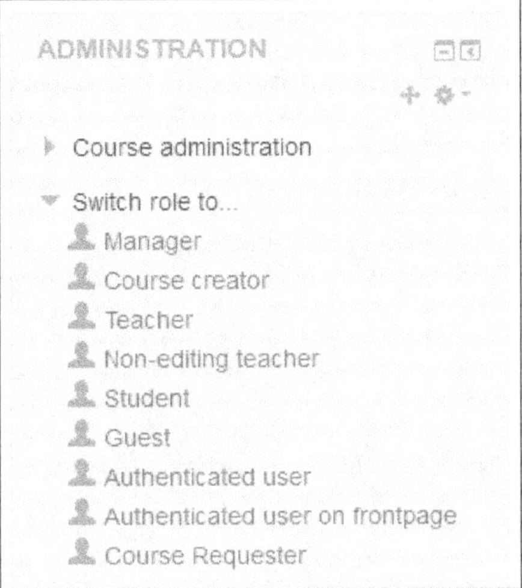

1. Create the new user by navigating to **Site administration** | **Users** | **Accounts** | **Add a new user**.
2. Assign your new user the role in the correct context, such as system roles or in a course as required.
3. Log in with this user in a different browser to check what they can do / see.

> Having two different roles logged in at the same time, each using a different browser, means that you can test the new role in one browser while still logged in as the administrator in your main browser. This saves so much time when building courses especially.

Manually adding a user to a course

Depending on what your role is on a course, you can add other users to the course by manually enrolling them to the course.

In this example, we are logged in as the administrator, which can add a number of roles, including:

- Manager
- Teacher
- Non-Editing Teacher
- Student

To enrol a user in your course:

1. Go to the **Course administration** menu in the **Administration** block.
2. Expand on the **User settings**.
3. Click on the **Enrolled users** link.

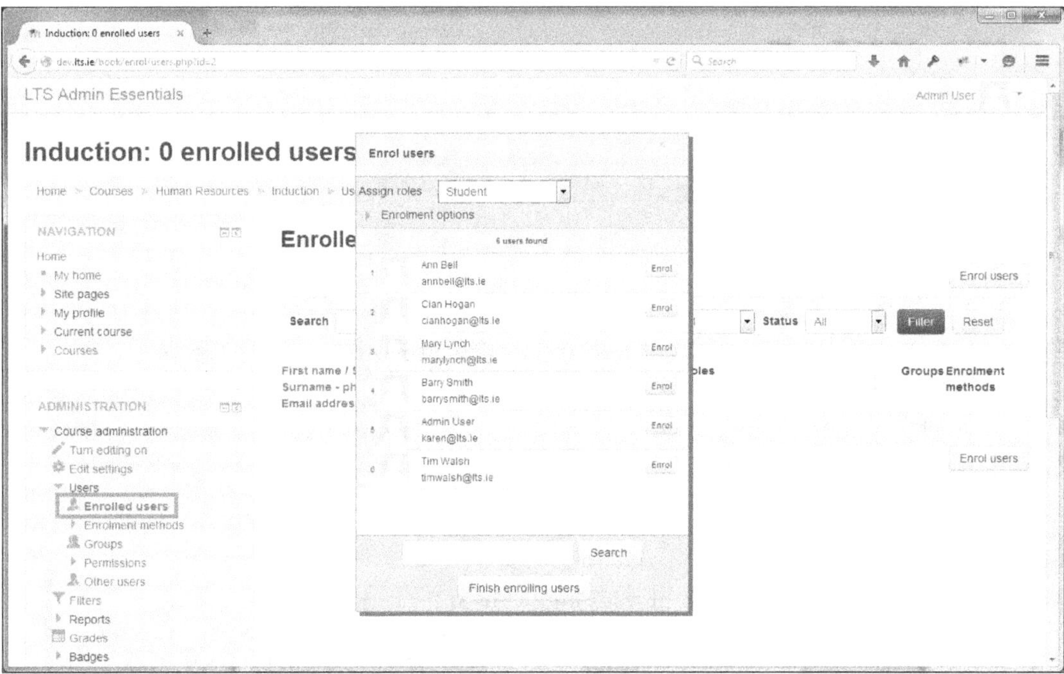

4. This brings up the enrolled users page that lists all enrolled users—this can be filtered by role and by default shows the enrolled participants only.
5. Click on the **Enrol users** button.
6. From the **Assign roles** dropdown, select which role you want to assign to the user. This is limited to the roles which you can assign.
7. Search for the user that you want to add to the course.
8. Click on the **Enrol** button to enroll the user with the assigned role.
9. Click on **Finish enrolling users**.

The page will now reload with the new enrolments. To see the users that you added with the given role, you may need to change the filter to the specific role type.

This is how you manually add someone to a Moodle course.

Alternatively, you can now extend user uploading for bulk enrolment as previously covered in *Chapter 2, Managing User Accounts and Authentication*. User upload CSV files allow you to include optional enrolment fields, which will enable you to enroll existing or new users. The sample user upload `csv` file will enroll each user as a student to both specified courses, identified by their course shortnames: Teaching with Moodle, and Induction.

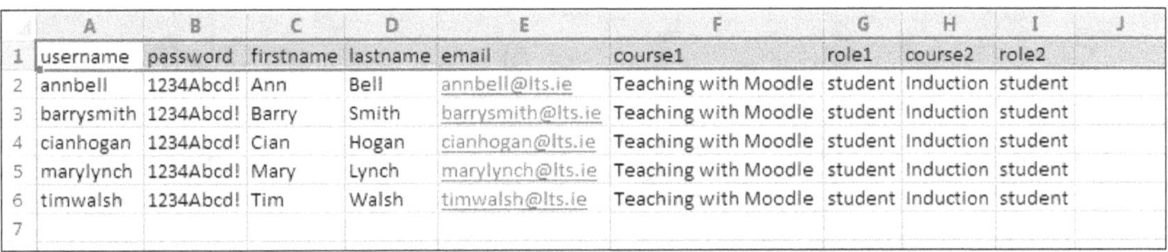

	A	B	C	D	E	F	G	H	I	J
1	username	password	firstname	lastname	email	course1	role1	course2	role2	
2	annbell	1234Abcd!	Ann	Bell	annbell@lts.ie	Teaching with Moodle	student	Induction	student	
3	barrysmith	1234Abcd!	Barry	Smith	barrysmith@lts.ie	Teaching with Moodle	student	Induction	student	
4	cianhogan	1234Abcd!	Cian	Hogan	cianhogan@lts.ie	Teaching with Moodle	student	Induction	student	
5	marylynch	1234Abcd!	Mary	Lynch	marylynch@lts.ie	Teaching with Moodle	student	Induction	student	
6	timwalsh	1234Abcd!	Tim	Walsh	timwalsh@lts.ie	Teaching with Moodle	student	Induction	student	
7										

Enabling self-enrolment for a course

In addition to manually adding users to a course, you can configure a course so that students can self-enroll onto the course, either with or without an enrolment key or password.

There are two dependencies required for this to work:

1. Firstly, the self-enrolment plugin needs to be enabled at the site level. This is found in the **Administration** block, by navigating to **Site Administration | Plugins | Enrolments | Manage enroll plugins**. If it is not enabled, you need to click on the eye icon to enable it. It is enabled by default in Moodle.

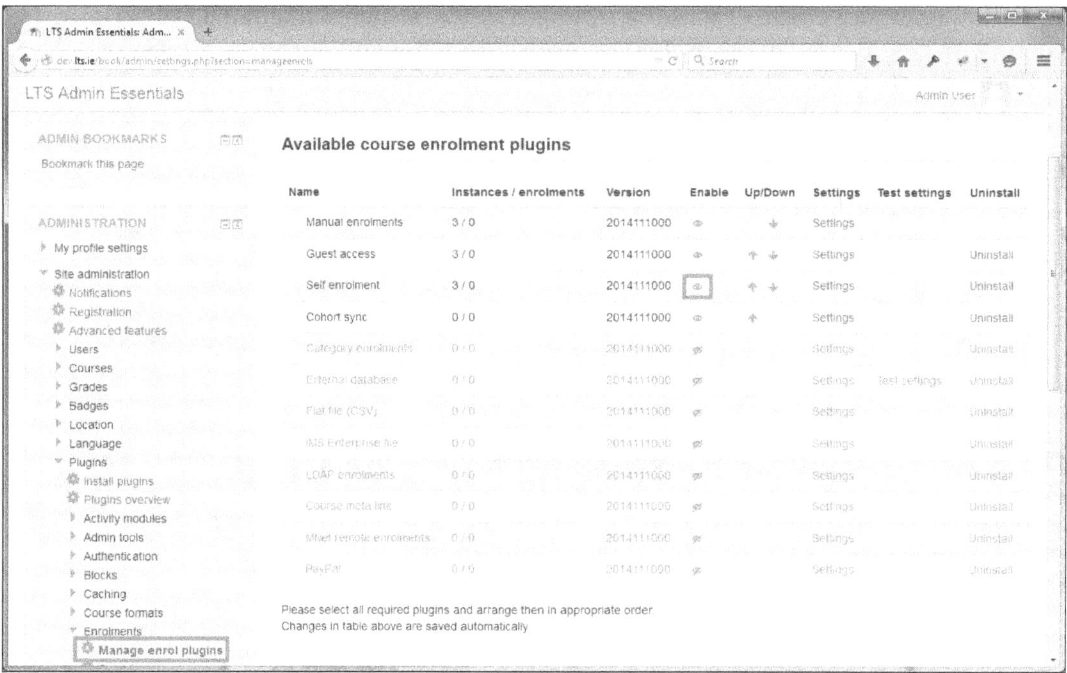

2. Secondly, you need to enable the self-enrolment method in the course itself, and configure it accordingly.

In the course that you want to enable self-enrolment, the following are the essential steps:

1. In the **Administration** block, navigate to **Administration | Course administration | Users | Enrolment methods**.
2. Click on the eye icon to turn on the **Self enrolment** method.

3. Click on the cogwheel icon to access the configuration for the **Self enrolment** method.

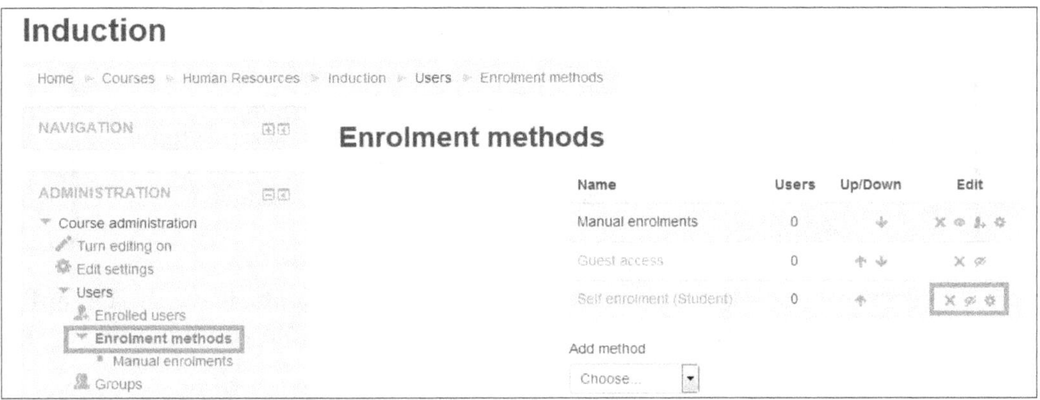

4. You can optionally enter a name for the method into the **Custom instance name** field; however, this is not required. Typically, you would do this if you are enabling multiple self-enrolment options and want to identify them separately:

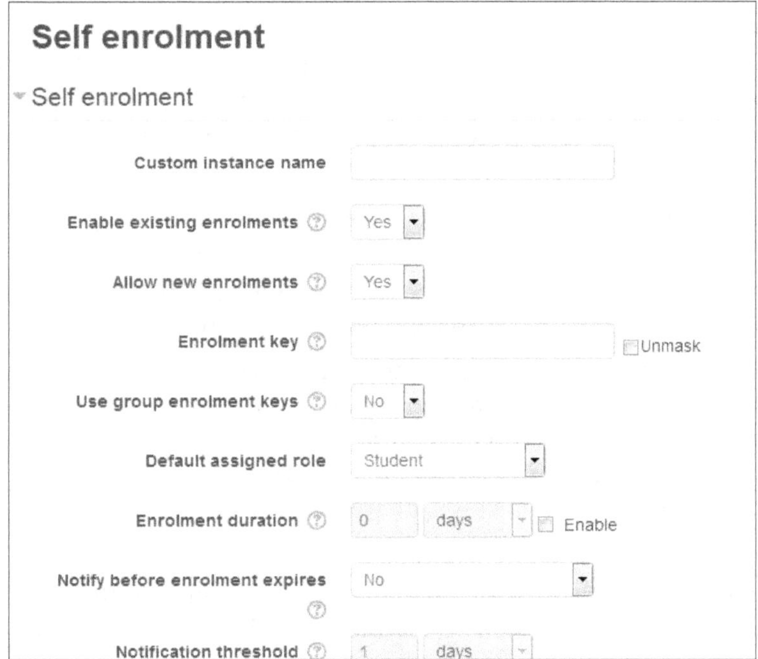

5. Enter an enrolment key or password into the **Enrolment key** field if you want to restrict self-enrolment to those who are issued the password. Once the user knows the password, they will be able to enroll.

If you are using groups in your course, and configure them with different passwords for each group, it is possible to use the **Use group enrolment keys** option to use those passwords from the different groups to automatically place the self-enrolling users into those groups when they enroll, using the correct key/password.

6. If you want the self-enrolment to enroll users as students, leave the **Default assigned role** as **Student**, or change it to whichever role you intend it to operate for.

Some organizations will give one password for the students to enrol with and another for the teachers to enrol with, so that the organization does not need to manage the enrolment centrally. So, having two self-enrolment methods set up, one pointing at student and one at teacher, makes this possible.

7. If you want to control the length of enrolment, you can do this by setting the **Enrolment duration** column. In this case, you can also issue a warning to the user before it expires by using **Notify before enrolment expires** and **Notification threshold** options.
8. If you want to specify the length of the enrolment, you can set this with **Start date** and **End date**.
9. You can un-enroll the user if they are inactive for a period of time by setting **Unenroll** to inactive after a specific number of days.
10. Set **Max enrolled users** if you want to limit the number of users using this specific password to enroll to the course. This is useful if you are selling a specific number of seats on the course.
11. This self-enrolment method may be restricted to members of a specified cohort only. You can enable this by selecting a cohort from the dropdown for the **Only cohort members** setting.
12. Leave **Send course welcome message** ticked if you want to send a message to those who self-enroll. This is recommended.

13. Enter a welcome message in the **Custom welcome message** field. This will be sent to all users who self-enroll using this method, and can be used to remind them of key information about the course, such as a starting date, or asking them to do something like complete the icebreaker in the course.
14. Click on **Save changes**.

Once enabled and configured, users will now be able to self-enroll and will be added as whatever role you selected. This is dependent on the course itself being visible to the users when browsing the site.

Other custom roles

Moodle docs has a list of potential custom roles with instructions on how to create them including:

- Parent
- Demo teacher
- Forum moderator
- Forum poster role
- Calendar editor
- Blogger
- Quiz user with unlimited time
- Question Creator
- Question sharer
- Course requester role
- Feedback template creator
- Grading forms publisher
- Grading forms manager
- Grade view
- Gallery owner role

For more information, check `https://docs.moodle.org/29/en/Creating_custom_roles`.

Summary

In this chapter, we looked at the core administrator tasks in role management, and the different aspects to consider when deciding which approach to take in either extending or reducing role permissions.

In the next chapter, we focus on factors to consider when adding and managing plugins on your Moodle site.

6
Managing Site Plugins

In the previous chapter, we looked at core administrator tasks in role management and the different aspects to consider when deciding which approach to take in either extending or reducing role permissions.

In this chapter, we will be examining ways to enhance the functionality of your Moodle site, by adding available plugins to the default Moodle install.

We also deal with the essential areas of site plugin management that every administrator may have to deal with:

- Sourcing a plugin
- Assessing a plugin for its suitability as a proposed solution
- Installing a plugin
- Updating a plugin
- Uninstalling a plugin

What are plugins?

As covered in an earlier chapter, Moodle is an acronym and the M in Moodle stands for Modular. For the most part, these modular features that are available in Moodle are all individual plugins or collections of plugins.

For example, the Quiz engine in Moodle that is used for the online tests is an activity plugin called **Quiz**. The questions that are used in the Quiz are plugins called Question types and how these can be configured to behave when students interact with them is controlled by a type of plugin called **Question behavior**.

Different plugins are available to install in Moodle to extend its functionality and appearance. The main types of plugins are listed here, and we will describe some of these in more detail later:

- Activity modules
- Admin tools
- Assignment submissions
- Assignment feedbacks
- Blocks
- Course formats
- Editor plugins
- External tool source
- Filters
- Gradebook plugins
- Plagiarism plugins
- Quiz and question plugins
- Reports
- Themes
- User tools, including authentication and enrolment

Where to find plugins

Within the Moodle interface, you will find the plugins management area in the administration block.

In the **Administration** block under **Site administration**, expand the **Plugins** section. This brings up three things: a link to **Install plugins**, a link to the **Plugins overview** page, and the expandable list of the top level plugins areas in Moodle.

Click on the **Plugins overview** page and it will bring up the list of all installed plugins, including the **Plugin name**, **Source** type, **Version** number, **Release** number, **Availability**, Link to **Settings** if available under **Actions**, Link to **Uninstall**, and any **Notes** related to the plugin such as dependencies.

Considerations when choosing a plugin

There are many third-party plugins available for Moodle. However, it is important to assess the suitability, reliability, and supportability of the plugin before adopting it. If you are using a third-party hosting company, such as a Moodle partner, they may have already audited the plugin so that it will be good to understand which aspects have been audited. Although something may be technically sound, the cost implications may require you to think of a different solution.

So, these are some of the criteria that one can use to evaluate a third-party Moodle plugin.

Initially, you need to question the basic purpose behind the suggested use of the plugin.

- **What is the purpose of the plugin?**

  Before installing any plugin to enhance Moodle, consider whether the implementation is merited or if the enhancement is duplicated in the standard plugins.

- **Is this the best solution for this requirement?**

  Whether there is no feature in your Moodle site already, or not, you should consider whether it is the best solution for the requirement. There are often multiple options available to achieve a specific requirement, and each should be considered before settling on one.

- **Is it easy to install?**

  At top level, if a plugin is complicated to install, is not just a simple plugin and perhaps needs extra server requirements, or even code changes to core Moodle to work, all these factors contribute to its complexity. So, this needs to be assessed to avoid long-term surprises.

- **Is the source managed on a Git repository?**

  Managing your codebase installation using Git is the best practice; therefore, it is preferable if the code for the plugin is also managed in this way, to make your installation and updates easier both initially and in the long term.

Git is a popular version control system that is used to manage software code. For more information on Git, check out `https://git-scm.com/`.

- **Is it available in the Moodle.org plugins database?**

  When a plugin is available in the Moodle.org plugin directory, it has gone through a level of checks that will make your technical assessment faster.

- **Is the documentation good?**

  Without good documentation, a plugin is just a piece of code that you will need to rely on looking at the code to see what it does, and relying on the interface for usage guidance. So, it is important to consider whether it has good documentation, including the following:

  - A Moodle Docs page
  - A good readme.txt
  - Instructional videos and help sheets
  - Good help files and instructions

  If there is insufficient documentation, you will need to consider what you need to create to assist your staff and end users.

- **Is it easy for teachers to use?**

  It is important to consider the ease of use for the teachers and course creators. Adoption of the plugin will depend on this and a complex tool or one that is confusing to use can increase the support calls on an administrator and support team. Good documentation can help in this area.

- **Are the instructions for use correct and usable?**

  Sometimes you may find that a plugin has documentation, but it may not be up-to-date. It may be for only some aspects of the tool and does not explain the usage fully. So, this should be assessed and fixed if needed.

- **Is it easy for a student to use?**

  If the plugin is for the students to use, usability is paramount. More so than for teachers, clear and obvious usage is important for students. It must do "what it says on the tin." It is a good idea to have students perform usability testing on new features before they go live.

- **Does it provide the functionality as described in a good sensible way, is it a "full feature" or an interim solution?**

  A big challenge is where the required functionality is a small part of a bigger plugin, or indeed the plugin meets only a small but key part of the requirement. This is where the overall complexity of the final solution has to be taken and compared to the complexity that is being introduced.

- **What features should be considered?**

  With any plugin, if you choose to adopt it rather than code your own solution, a key consideration must be if it has a roadmap of potential improvements /changes going forward. If you come to depend on a new plugin and it stands still and has no roadmap, you get what you choose. However, if it has planned changes, would these render your planned usage problematic? This should be considered in your decision.

- **Will it work on a mobile device?**

  As Moodle is now a mobile-first course management system, in that the default themes are responsive (more and clean), therefore you need to consider responsive aspects in the plugin assessment as well.

  Some plugins, by their nature, may not suit mobile and responsive design, so you will need to consider what weighting this requirement is given in your analysis. We will recommend at least having it work on mobile device browsers.

- **What are the reviews?**

  Looking to see what other users are saying about the plugin is a good way to assess whether it is going to cause problems or not. Check the `https://moodle.org/` plugin entry for any comments from users on the plugin site or the `https://moodle.org/` forums for any discussions about the plugin. The `https://moodle.org/` site also sometimes has reviews of plugins, or if not check out some of the community sites such as `http://www.somerandomthoughts.com/blog/` that have plugin reviews.

- **What is the author's background (experience/reliability)?**

  Checking the experience and reliability of the author(s) with respect to the plugin is essential. You can check if they are active on the Moodle community for a good period of time, if they are new, or if they were active, but now are not. You should check whether they respond well to queries on bugs or issues of usage. This is to help ascertain whether you will get assistance when using the plugin or not.

  You should consider if they work for an established Moodle development team (a Moodle partner, or Moodle HQ, for example—although there are others too). This will mean that the plugin is likely to have been developed and maintained as part of their job and therefore more likely to be maintained going forward.

- **What are the financial considerations?**

  A plugin is for life and not just for installation! The costs of having a plugin installed are on-going through the increased resources for usage—be it disk space, database usage, or bandwidth, increased costs for testing for upgrades, patches, and potentially having to maintain it if the plugin author goes away. This total cost of ownership needs to be carefully assessed. Depending on the type of plugin, there may be cost implication to adoption of the plugin regarding a license or a commercial support contract for the plugin to ensure patches for upgrades and security fixes.

  There are guidelines for Moodle development, which ought to be followed by plugin developers. This is a list of some of the technical checks that one may want to include in your assessment of the plugin.

  - Does it work properly with the database types that you use?
  - Is the plugin being updated regularly with new Moodle version, and does it work with your one now, or the one you may update to?
  - Does the module follow good Moodle coding standards?
  - Does it properly use language files or has it got hardcoded text?
  - Does it properly follow accessibility guidelines?
  - Does it properly follow css and theming approaches?
  - Does it conflict with anything else naming wise?
  - Does it impact performance of Moodle in normal or high traffic usage?
  - What resources will it require to be used?
  - Does backup/restore/duplicate work?
  - Has it got unit tests?

Installing plugins

There are different methods for installing external plugins on your Moodle site, which are:

- Via the Moodle interface
    - Manually installing a plugin `ZIP` file
    - Installing a plugin from the Moodle plugin directory
- Via command line directly from the source control repository

Manually installing a plugin ZIP file

You will need to have a zipped file of the plugin code files. The hosting server will also need to be enabled with the correct write permissions for the directory (called folders in Windows OS) where the plugin will be installed.

For instance, if the plugin is a `block` plugin, the web server needs to be able to write to the `/block/` directory in the moodle directory. Once the plugin has been installed, the `/block/` directory permissions may then be returned to their original configuration if needed.

To manually install a plugin `ZIP` file:

1. Go to **Administration** block by navigating to **Site administration** | **Plugins** | **Install plugins**, which brings up the Plugin installer page.
2. Ignore the **Install plugins from the Moodle plugins directory** button for now, as this will be covered in the next section.
3. Select the relevant **Plugin type**, which you are installing.

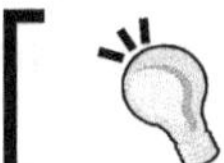

Note that a helpful error will instantly show if the selected destination directory is not writable as required.

4. For the `ZIP` package, in the file picker, select the plugin `ZIP` file from its current location or drag and drop the file into the drop box to add it.

5. Check the **Acknowledgement** checkbox to confirm that you understand, the security, and resilience implications to installing the plugin:

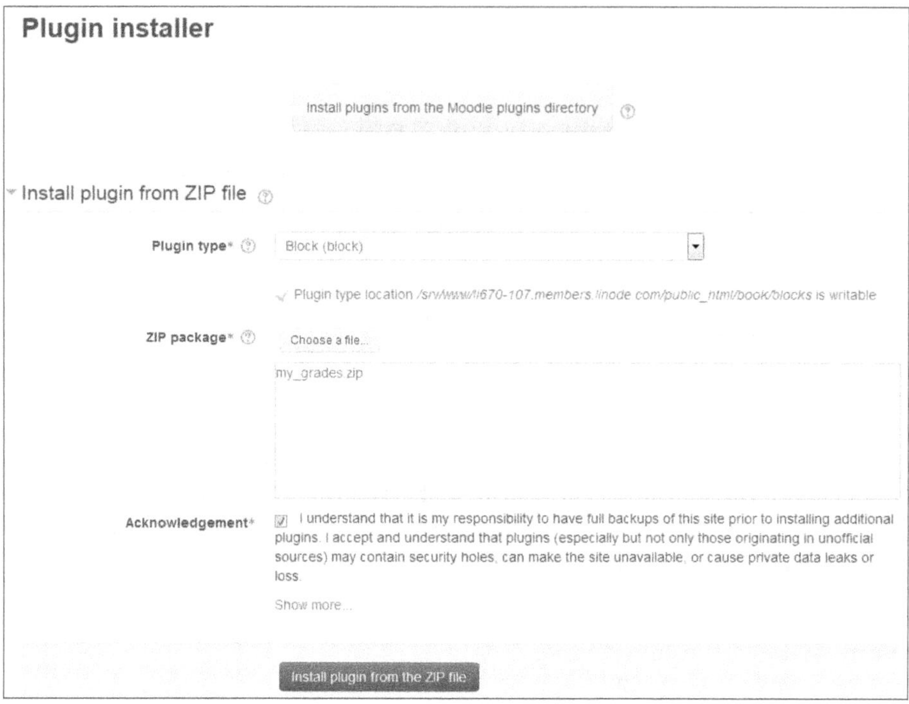

6. Click on **Install plugin from the ZIP file**.
7. The plugin `ZIP` file is now processed by a validation check. Once this check is passed, it allows you to either click on **Cancel** or **Install plugin!** to continue the process.
8. You will then see the Plugins check page with your plugin listed with a status of **To be installed**. This page will also list any other external plugins, which you have installed with their current status.
9. Click on **Upgrade Moodle database now**.
10. You should see a confirmation page with your plugin listed with its status as **Success**.

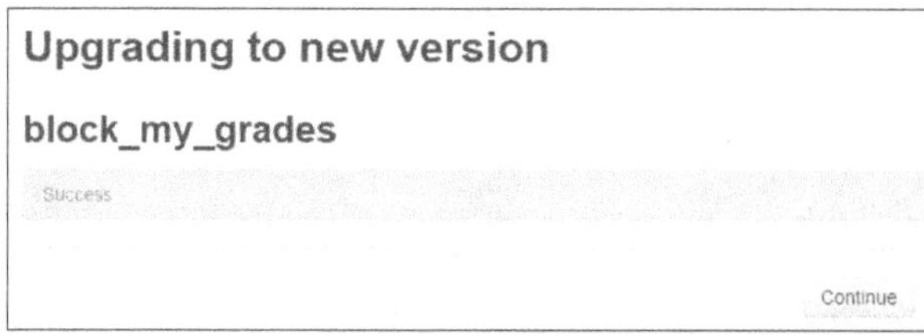

Note that if there are any errors being displayed on this final page, it may indicate if there are any issues with the plugin and its ongoing impact on your Moodle site, even though it is successfully installed.

11. Click on **Continue**.
12. If a plugin has any global settings configured, their edit page will now display with any default values pre-set, and can be updated and / or saved at this point with a click on **Save changes**. These values can be edited later at any time, which will be covered in the Editing plugin settings section.

Installing a plugin from the Moodle plugins directory

To install a plugin from the Moodle plugins directory without an `https://moodle.org/` login:

1. Go to **Administration** block by navigating to **Site administration** | **Plugins** | **Install plugins**. This brings up the Plugin installer page as before.
2. Click on **Install plugins from the Moodle plugins directory**:

3. Click on **Browse plugins**.
4. Locate the relevant plugin using the **Search** facility, or by clicking on the relevant plugin type, such as **Blocks** or **Themes**.
5. Click on the plugin name to view the plugin page.

6. Click on **Download** to download the plugin `ZIP` file.

Make sure that you are downloading the correct file for your Moodle site as plugins may have different files for different Moodle released versions.

7. You now have a plugin `ZIP` file, which you can now install on your moodle site as per the steps in the previous section.

To install a plugin from the Moodle plugins directory with an `https://moodle.org/` login:

1. Go to **Administration** block by navigating to **Site administration** | **Plugins** | **Install plugins**. This brings up the Plugin installer page as before.
2. Click on **Install plugins from the Moodle plugins directory**.
3. Click on **Log in**.
4. Type in your **Username** and **Password** and click on **Log in**.
5. Locate the relevant plugin using the **Search** facility, or by clicking on the relevant plugin type, such as **Blocks** or **Themes**.
6. Click on the plugin name to view the plugin page:

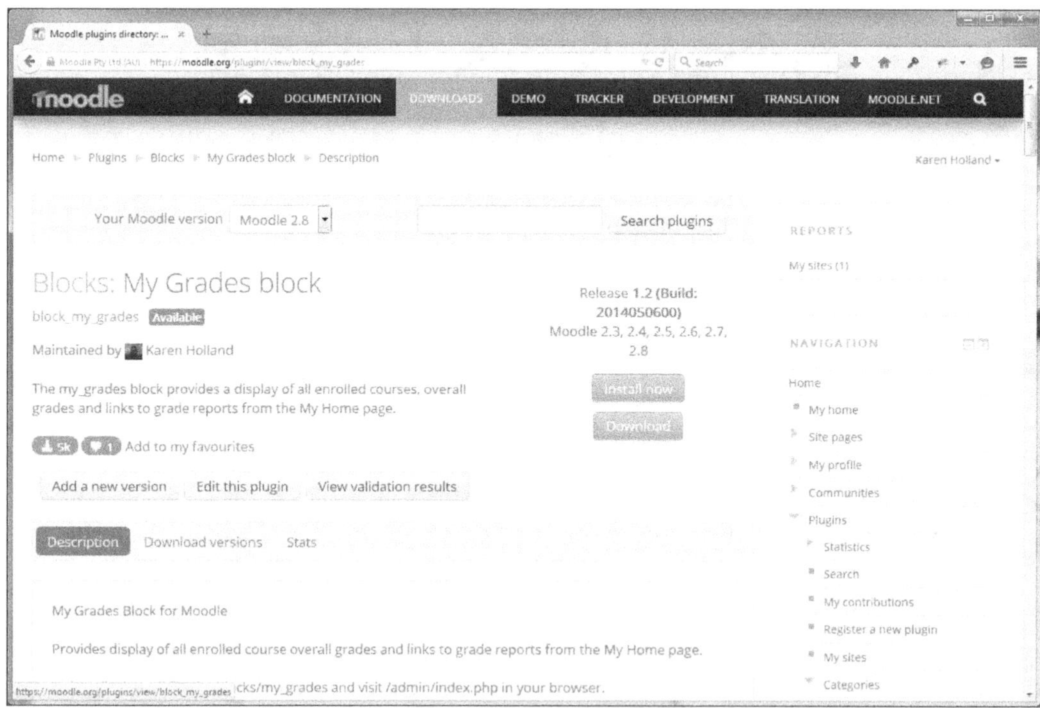

7. Click on **Install now** to initiate the direct installation process.
8. Your moodle site is now listed in **My site page**.
9. Click on the **Install now** link for your relevant moodle site to install your plugin.
10. This will return you to your moodle site to a confirmation page to install the plugin, displaying its details, such as its version ID.
11. Click on **Continue**.
12. This now processes the plugin validation check. Once this check is passed, this allows you to click on **Cancel** or click on **Install plugin!** to continue the process.
13. You will then see the **Plugins check** page with your plugin listed with a status of **To be installed**. This page will also list any other external plugins, which you installed with their current status.
14. Click on **Upgrade Moodle database now**.
15. You should see a confirmation page with your plugin listed with its status as **Success**:

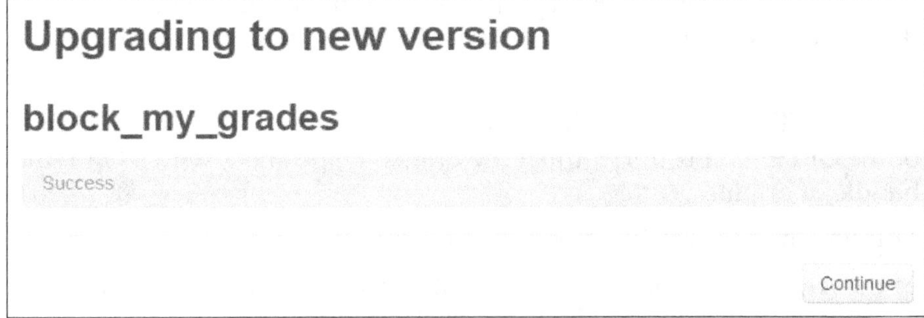

Note that if there are any errors being displayed on this final page, it may indicate that there are any issues with the plugin and its ongoing impact on your Moodle site, even though it has been successfully installed.

16. Click on **Continue**.
17. If a plugin has any global settings configured, their edit page will now be displayed with any default values pre-set, and can be updated and / or saved at this point with a click on **Save changes**. These values can be edited later at any time, which will be covered in the **Editing plugin** settings section.

Installing a plugin from a source control URL

To install a plugin from a source control URL, in this example, `https://github.com/`:

1. SSH into your Moodle server.
2. Go to your moodle site folder.
3. Go to the relevant directory for the plugin type to be installed, such as **blocks**, bearing in mind that the web server needs to be able to write to this directory. Once the plugin has been installed, the relevant directory permissions may then be returned to their original configuration if needed.
4. Locate the source control URL for the relevant plugin. The Moodle plugin directory lists this URL in the relevant plugin page's **Useful links** section if supplied by the plugin maintainer.
5. Type in the following command line:

```
git clone
https://github.com/learningtechnologyservices/moodle-block_my_
grades.git my_grades
```

Note that you may need to specify a branch for your plugin clone, depending on the plugin code needed for your Moodle site version.

6. This should create a new directory called `my_grades`, which is a full clone of the GitHub repository or just the branch if specified, with a Git remote handle of origin.
7. You now need to log into your Moodle site as admin.
8. In the **Administration** block under **Site administration**, click on **Notifications** to bring up the **Plugins check** page, which will list the plugin that you have just uploaded to the server via Git.
9. Click on **Upgrade Moodle database now**.
10. You should see a confirmation page with your plugin listed with its status as **Success**.

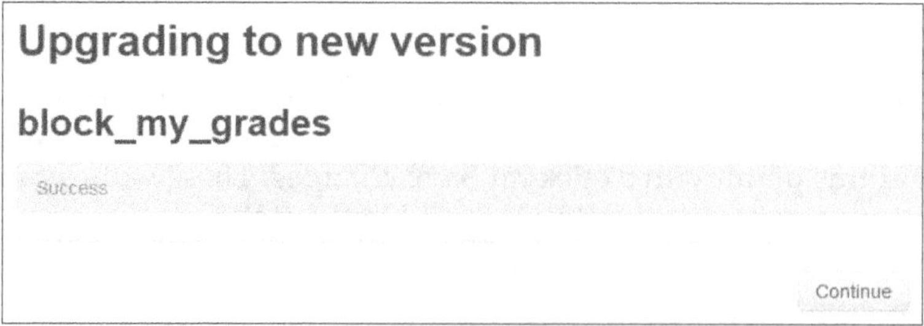

Please note that if there are any errors being displayed on this final page, it may indicate that there are any issues with the plugin and its potential impact on your Moodle site, even though it has successfully installed.

11. Click on **Continue**.
12. If a plugin has any global settings configured, their edit page will now display with any default values pre-set, and can be updated and / or saved at this point with a click on **Save changes**. These values can be edited later at any time, which will be covered in the **Editing** plugin settings section.

Editing plugin settings

To edit the settings of a plugin, if they exist:

1. Go to **Administration** block by navigating to **Site administration** | **Plugins** | **Plugins overview**, which brings up the Plugins overview page.
2. Click on **Show additional plugins only**. This filters the list to only show additional installed plugins.
3. Click on the **Settings** link for the relevant plugin, in this case **Progress Bar**:

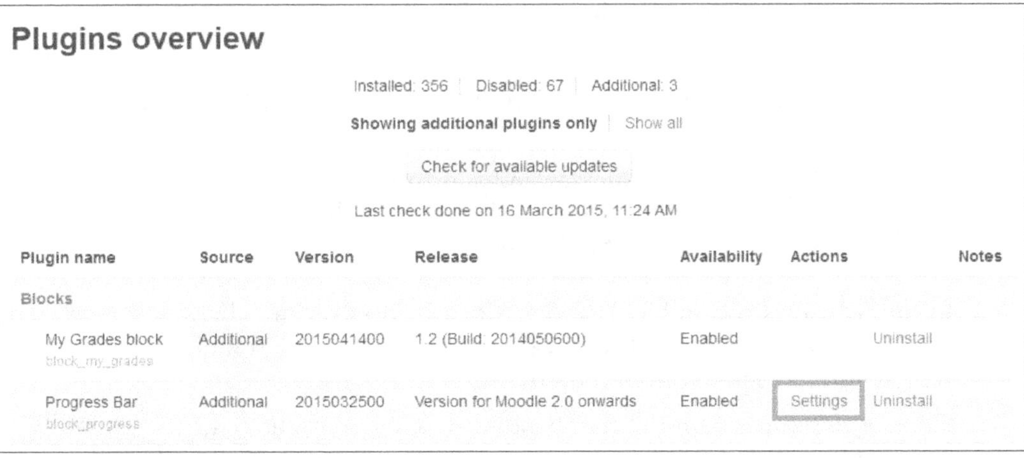

4. Alternatively, you can reach the Progress Bar settings page under **Administration** | **Site administration** | **Plugins** | **Blocks** | **Progress Bar** where **Blocks** is your plugin type and **Progress Bar** is your plugin name.

5. You may now edit any of the plugin settings as required. Any default values are also displayed.
6. Click on **Save changes**.

Updating plugins

Your Moodle site automatically tracks any relevant version updates or patches to installed plugins on the Moodle plugins database. This is done via the Notifications page.

For updated plugin code from other sources, you need to SSH to the relevant plugin folder, manually add the new code there and follow the steps below from step 5 onwards.

To update a plugin from the Moodle plugins database, perform the following:

1. In the **Administration** block under **Site administration**, click on **Notifications** and click on the **plugins overview** link, which displays if any updated plugins are detected.
2. Alternatively, in the **Administration** block navigating to **Site administration** | **Plugins** | **Plugins overview** also brings up the **Plugins overview** page, which will list any available updated plugins.
3. Click on the relevant **Download** link.
4. Save the zipped plugin file.
5. SSH to the relevant plugin folder and then manually add the new code.

Please note that this step and onwards can also be achieved for updated plugin code, which is from a different source to the Moodle plugins database.

6. In the **Administration** block under **Site administration**, click on **Notifications** to bring up the **Plugins check** page, which will list the plugin which you have just updated on the server.
7. Click on **Upgrade Moodle database now**. This is essential, as the updated plugin may have different database requirements to the original plugin.
8. You should see a confirmation page with your plugin listed with a status of Success.

Uninstalling plugins

To uninstall a plugin:

1. Go to **Administration** block by navigating to **Site administration** | **Plugins** | **Plugins overview**, which brings up the **Plugins overview** page.
2. Click on **Show additional plugins only**. This filters the list to only show additional installed plugins.
3. Click on the **Uninstall** link for the relevant plugin, in this case **Progress Bar**.

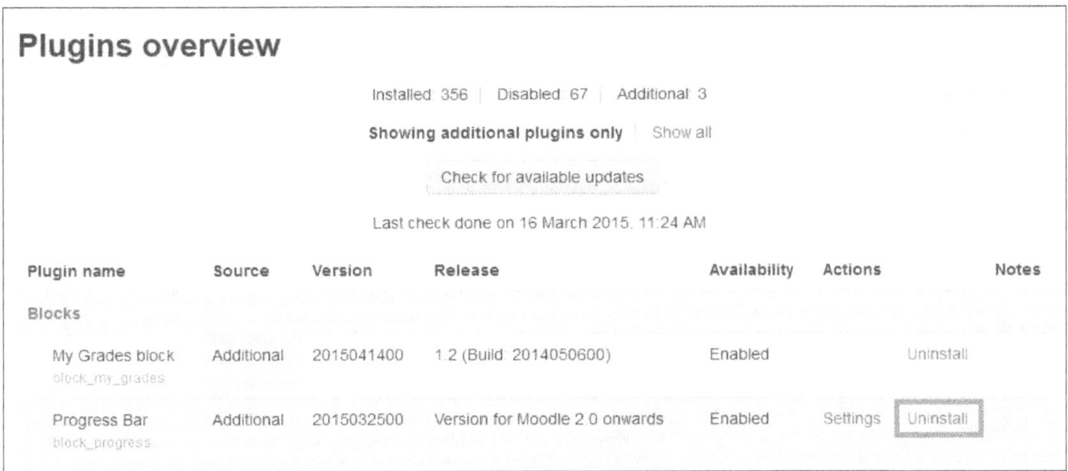

4. Click on **Continue** to complete the uninstallation process. If the web server has delete permissions for the plugin directory, it will now be removed. Otherwise, the plugin directory will need to be removed directly from the server to avoid it being reinstalled again.

[Please note that uninstalling a plugin will remove all associated data and cannot be undone.]

Summary

In this chapter, we focused on the management of additional plugins on the Moodle site, and how the site can be customized to include more functionality and features for all users.

We looked at the different methods of installing plugins, either by installing them via the Moodle interface itself or using SSH access to the Moodle server to upload the code from a source control URL such as `https://github.com/`. We also looked at how to edit the plugin settings if required and also how to update the plugin when and as needed.

In the next chapter, we will be looking at the issue of how to deal with end of year course rollovers and what processes and procedures are needed and are suitable for your particular usage of Moodle.

7
End of Year Course Rollover

In the previous chapter, we looked at how to add and manage plugins on your Moodle site. The next question that administrators have to handle is how to deal with courses and course content, where one intake of students has finished, and the site needs to be prepared for a fresh intake of students. This process needs to be planned, agreed, and implemented among administrators, teachers, and other relevant stakeholders.

In this context, stakeholders refer to all interested parties in the learning management system including faculties, departments, student bodies such as student unions, IT departments, and learning units.

In this chapter, we deal with the essential areas of the end of year course rollover management that every administrator will have to deal with, as follows:

- Agreeing on a rollover procedure
- End of course final backup
- Course restore
- Course reset

Rollover implementation

There are a number of factors to consider when deciding on the most suitable rollover procedure to follow:

- Who creates the course format and content
- Whether the old courses will still need to be accessible to teachers or students
- The volume of the courses involved

- The amount of downtime required to create the backups and how this will affect user access
- Whether all courses stop/start at the same time

The basic three types of rollover procedures are as follows:

- Backup the entire Moodle site and host it at a different URL
- Backup the relevant courses with their full user data and restore them as new entities without the user data
- Backup the relevant courses with their full user data, and reset the original courses so that they no longer contain any user data

Backup of the entire Moodle site

A full site backup may only be done by administrators with full access to the server command line, not via the Moodle interface itself.

The administrator will take a backup of the database, the moodle web files, and the `config.php` and `moodledata` folder. They will then install this to a different URL than the original site, for example `www.example.com/2014` or `2014.example.com`, and then migrate the content to the new URL.

This process is not covered in this book.

For further details on this procedure, please read the Moodle documentation at `https://docs.moodle.org/28/en/Site_backup`.

Duplication of courses in the same Moodle after backups

Duplication of the courses in the same Moodle involves backing up, and then restoring each course into the category structure.

Two of the distinct choices available are as follows:

- Maintaining the same category structure and naming each course for the new semester year with the year included, such as Maths101_2014, Maths101_2015.
- Duplicating the whole category structure and putting the new courses into the new structure so that the site has a 2014 and 2015 top level category.

Variations of these approaches are also common.

Taking a backup of a Moodle course can be done via the Moodle interface with either a manual process per course, or by setting up an automated course backup. Refer to the *Course Backup* section of this chapter for further information.

The courses are then restored into the new location and given a new name. The courses are usually restored without student enrolments or student created data, such as forum posts, assignments, and grades. This then leaves the course ready for the new intake of students.

Resetting courses after a backup

Resetting the existing courses in the Moodle site has the benefit of not needing to create duplicates and keeps the site clean with just the needed courses for that year.

It is good practice to take backups of the courses for archival purposes. This includes creating the Moodle course backup, downloading it to your desktop, storing it on your standard storage system that is secure and used for archival purposes. As before, the backup of a Moodle course can be done via the Moodle interface, with either a manual process per course or by setting up an automated course backup.

Once backups are taken for long-term storage, the resetting is carried out via the Moodle interface.

The manual process for resetting a course backup is explained in more detail in *Reset of courses after backup* section later in this chapter.

Once reset, the courses have no student data and are ready for the next intake of students. The course content, activities, blocks, structure, gradebook, and settings are all still in the course. It is just the student data that is removed in a typical reset. Remember, you control what is removed during the reset process.

Selecting the right approach

Each of these approaches have their pros and cons and it depends on the resources and time available to the administrator and staff as to which approach is taken.

As a general rule, if live access is not required to old courses, then taking archival backups of the site or courses and resetting the finished courses is the most practical approach.

Course backup

Making a manual backup of a course in Moodle will depend on your account permissions in that course.

Teacher permissions in course backup

If you are an editing teacher of a course, you are able to:

1. Make a backup of any of your courses, selecting which content and additional plugin configurations to include.
2. Download the backup file of the course in its `.mbz` format, allowing you to archive it elsewhere, so that it can be restored for later use.

Course creator permissions in course backup

If you are a course creator on the Moodle site, you are able to:

1. Make a backup of any of the courses that you have access to, selecting which content and additional plugin configurations to include.
2. Download the backup file of the course in its `.mbz` format, allowing you to archive it elsewhere, so that it can be restored for later use.

Administrator permissions in course backup

If you are an administrator on the Moodle site, you have far more flexibility in your ability to backup courses, being able to:

1. Make a backup of any of the courses on the Moodle site, selecting which content and additional plugin configurations to include.
2. Include any selected user data in the course backup, including enrolled users, user submitted content, user grades, which may be anonymized if required.
3. Download the backup file of the course in its `.mbz` format, allowing you to archive it elsewhere so that it can be restored for later use.

Making a backup of a course

To back up a course in Moodle, you must be logged into the Moodle course with a user that has sufficient privileges to make a backup of that course:

1. In the **Administration** block under **Course administration** menu, click on **Backup**.

2. Select the activities, blocks, filters, badges, and other items to be included in the course backup.
3. As an administrator, you can also choose which user data to include in the backup, such as enrolled users, user roles, groups, user submissions, user files, user logs, and grades. You can also specify whether all the user data should be anonymized or not:

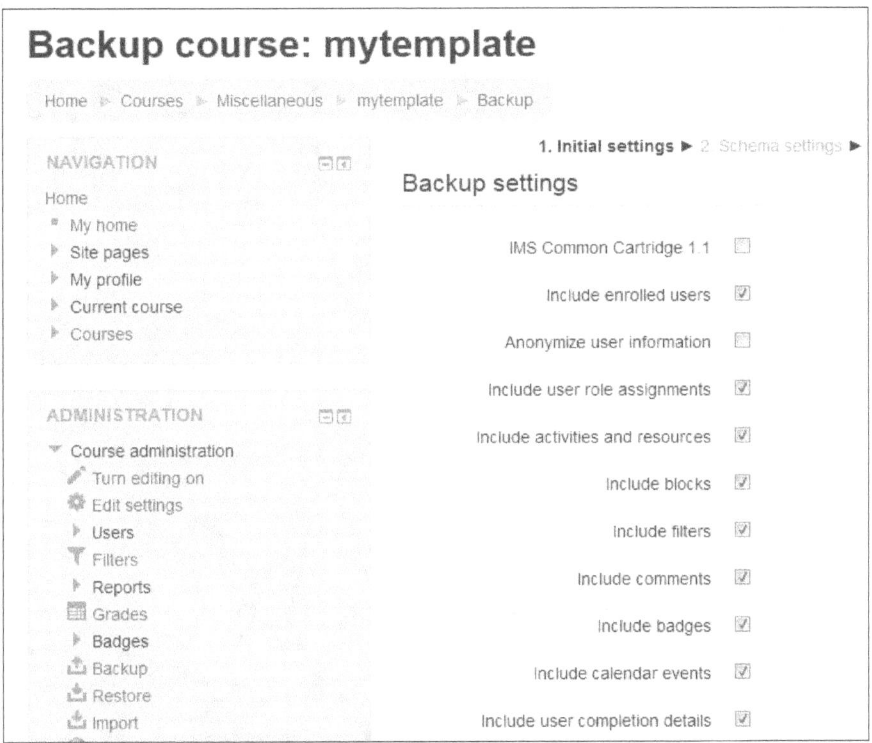

4. Click on **Next**.
5. Review the activities and resources to be included in the backup. Deselect specific items as needed, depending on the purpose of the backup, and click on **Next** to continue.
6. The backup filename can be customized to a more meaningful name if required. For example, I always add my initials to the start of the backup file name so that it is identifiable as one of my backups:

Filename

Filename* backup-moodle2-course-5-mytemplate-20150314-0

7. Check that everything is as required, then click on the **Perform backup** button.
8. Click on the **Continue** button.
9. To download the backup file for safekeeping, click on the **Download** link.
10. To begin the restore process if needed, click on the **Restore** link.
11. The course backup is now created in Moodle and is accessible via the course restore interface:

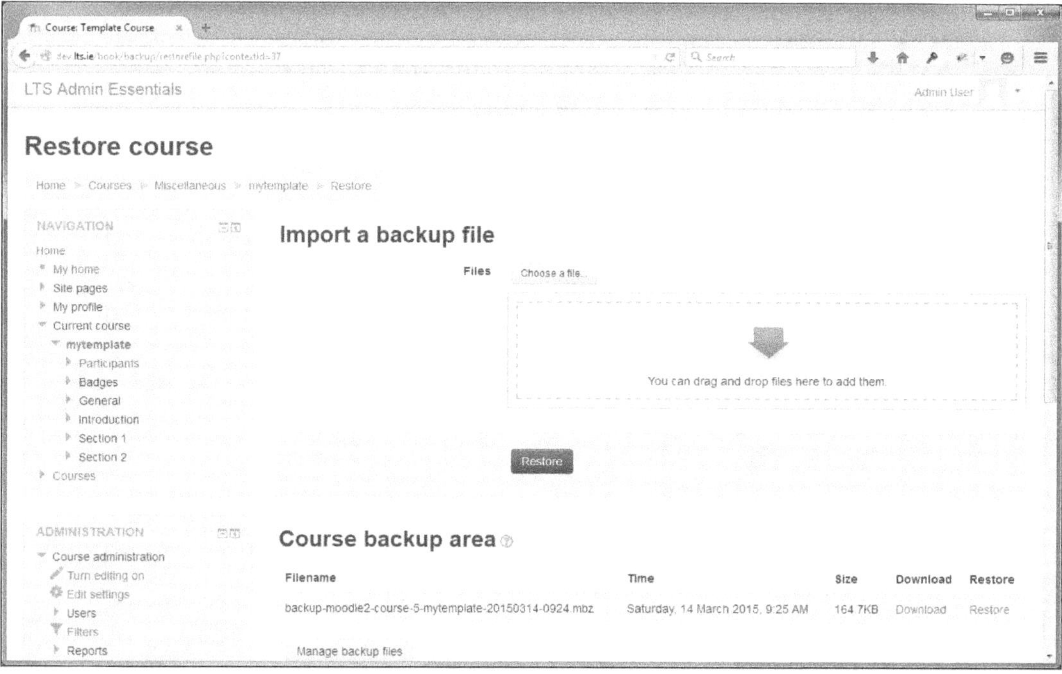

Setting up automated course backups

Administrators can configure Moodle so that courses are automatically backed up on a regular basis if they have changed.

To set up an automated course backup, perform the following:

1. In the **Administration** block, navigate to **Site administration** | **Courses** | **Backups** and click on **Automated backup setup**:

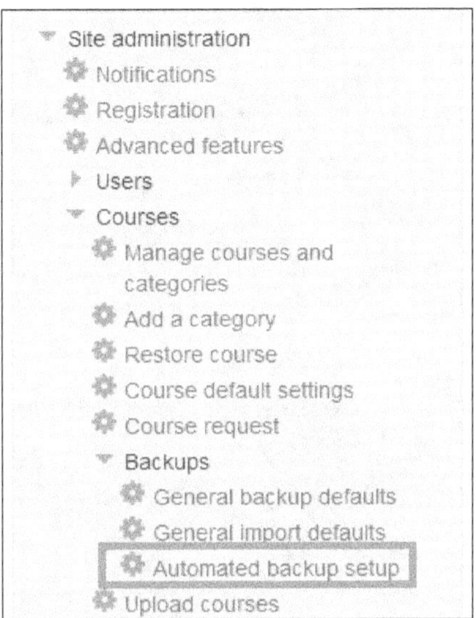

2. Set **Active** to `Enabled`.
3. Configure the **Schedule** day or days.
4. Select what **Execute at** time to run the automated backups, bearing in mind that this should ideally be done when the moodle site is least used, normally early morning.
5. Select the relevant **Automated backup storage** option you want for the location of your backup files.
    - **Course backup filearea**
    - **Specified directory for automated backups**
    - **Course backup filearea and the specified directory**, which then backs up to both locations

6. Set the full path to the specified directory required, as **Save to** value. This is recommended, as it allows you to make backups on a separate server in case your hosting server hardware fails and is unrecoverable:

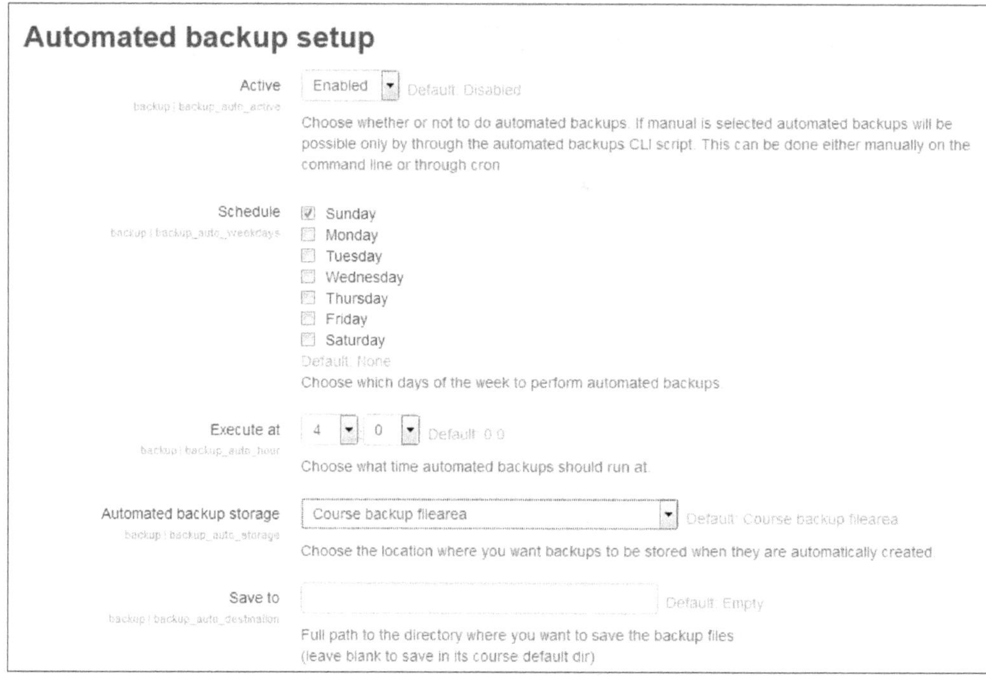

7. Click on **Use course name in backup filename**, as this makes identifying the specific course backups easier.
8. Choose whether to skip certain courses, such as hidden courses, or ones not modified either since the previous backup or within a specified number of days.
9. Click on the **Save changes** button.
10. When moodle cron runs, it will create the backups at the specified times. If you have selected for them to be saved into the `Course backup file area`, they will be available in **Restore course interface**, under the **Automated backups** section, which will be explained in more detail in the *Course Restore* section:

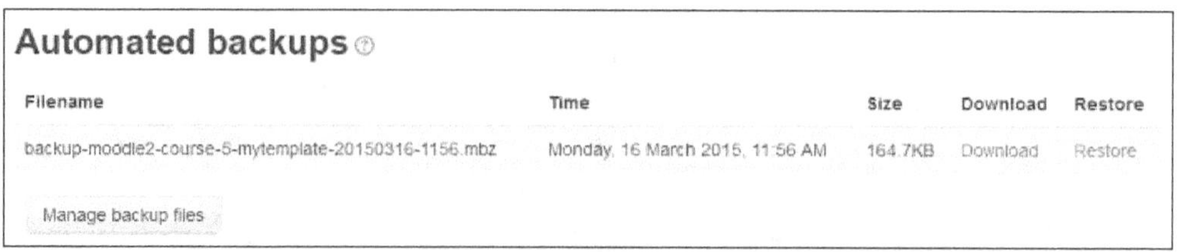

11. Alternatively, you can manually initiate the same process via command line, by running the `> php automated_backups.php from the /moodle/admin/cli` folder.

Please note that saving the automated course backups to a specific directory provides the administrator with a filesystem location that they can then backup to an external drive, or rsync to a network attached backup drive.

Course restore

Restoring a course in Moodle first of all depends on your account permissions.

Teacher permissions in course restore

If you are an editing teacher of a course, you are able to restore a backup file either into one of your existing courses, or into a new course that will need to be created for you by an administrator or course creator.

Course creator permissions in course restore

If you are a course creator on the Moodle site, you are able to restore a backup file either into one of the existing courses, or into a new course, which you can dynamically create during the restoration process.

Administrator permissions in course restore

If you are an administrator on the Moodle site, you have far more flexibility in your ability to restore courses, being able to restore a backup file either into one of the existing courses, or into a new course that you can dynamically create during the restoration process.

Restoring a course

The following are the steps for restoring a course:

1. Log in as an administrator level user account.
2. Access the **Restore course** options in the **Administration** block, by navigating to **Site administration** | **Courses** | **Restore course**.

3. Alternatively, go to the relevant course and click on **Administration** | **Course administration** | **Restore** if you want to restore from that specific course's backup file or files:

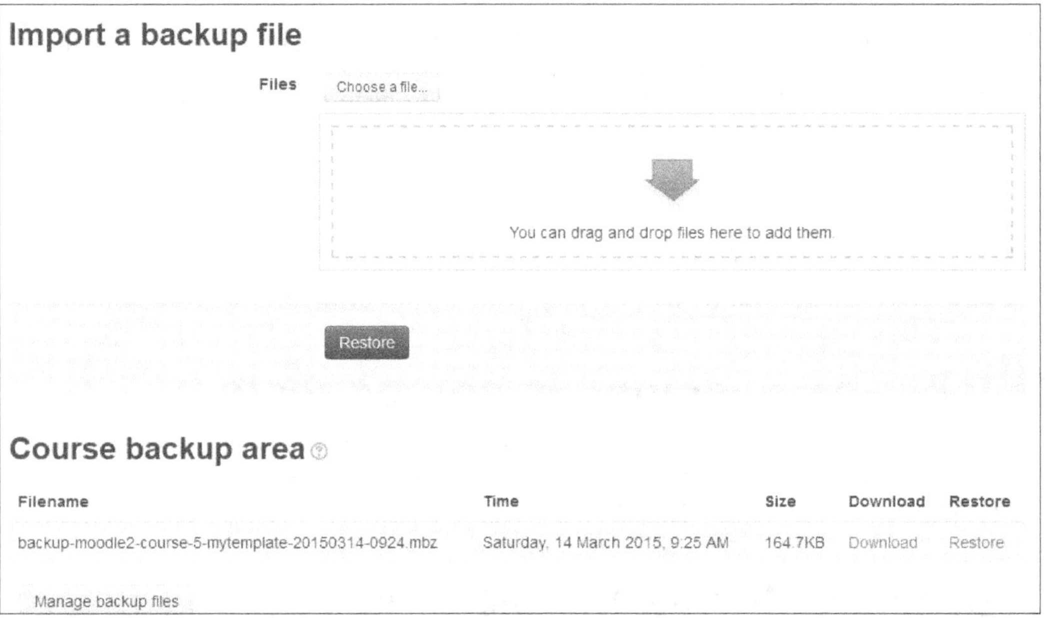

4. From here, there are two ways to begin the restore process, of which either one can be selected:
   - Click on **Choose a file** to upload the backup file and click on **Restore** below the file upload area.
   - Choose a file in **Course backup area** or **User private backup area** and click on the **Restore** link to the right of the file.
5. Check that everything is as required and then click on the **Continue** button.
6. At this point, with your administrator permissions, you can choose whether the course should be restored as a new course, or into an existing course.

7. To restore into a new course, choose the relevant category in which to add it and then click on the **Continue** button in the **Restore** as a new course section:

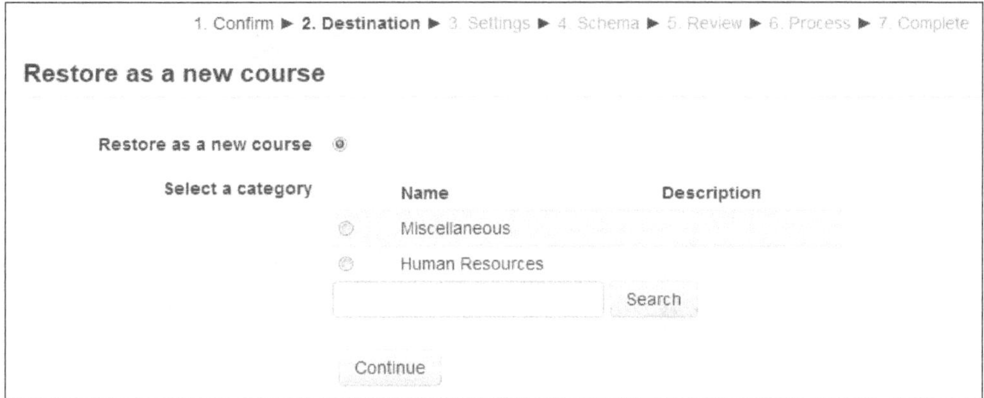

8. To restore into the present course, if you started the process in a course, choose whether to merge the backup into the course, or to delete the current course contents. Then, restore and click on the **Continue** button in the **Restore** into this course section.

> Please note that merging one course backup into another course can result in duplicate activities and resources so take care.

9. Select the activities, blocks, filters, and other items to be restored, and then click on the **Next** button in the lower right corner.

10. Amend the **Course name, short name,** and **start date** if necessary and review the items to be restored. Deselect any items you do not wish to have restored. Click on **Next** to continue.

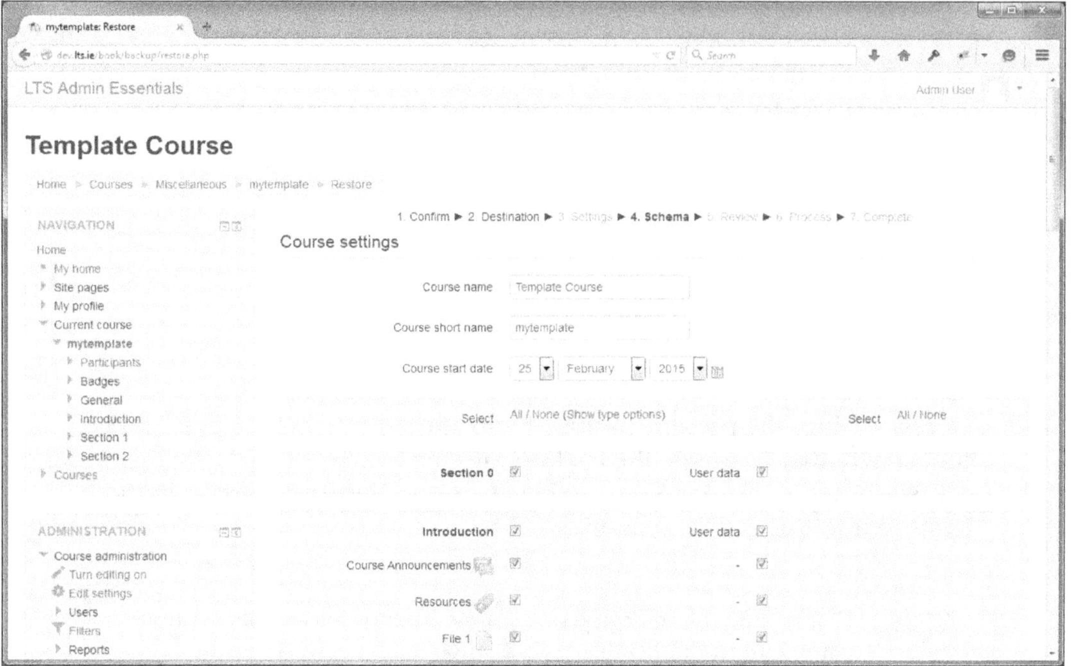

11. Check that everything is as required, then click on the **Perform** restore button.
12. A progress bar will display. Once the restore has completed, click on the **Continue** button.

The course is now restored in Moodle.

Please note that when restoring into courses with fewer sections than the original course, the activities from the additional sections will be orphaned activities in the new course. These orphaned activities will not be allocated to a live section in the course, so they will not be visible to students.

Course reset

This allows you to reset a course so that it contains its existing general content, such as activities and configurations, while emptying it of all user data:

1. Log in as an administrator level user account.
2. Access the course management options in the **Administration** block by navigating to **Course administration** | **Reset**:

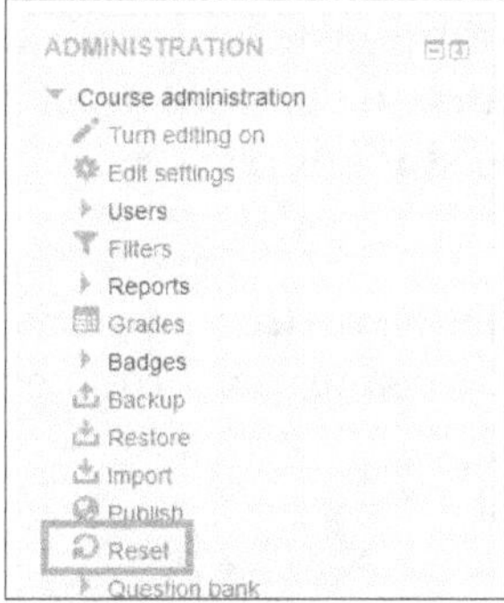

3. Enable the **Course** start date for editing if you wish to change it.
4. Click on the **Expand** all link to view all of the course data, and select the activities and other items that you want emptied:

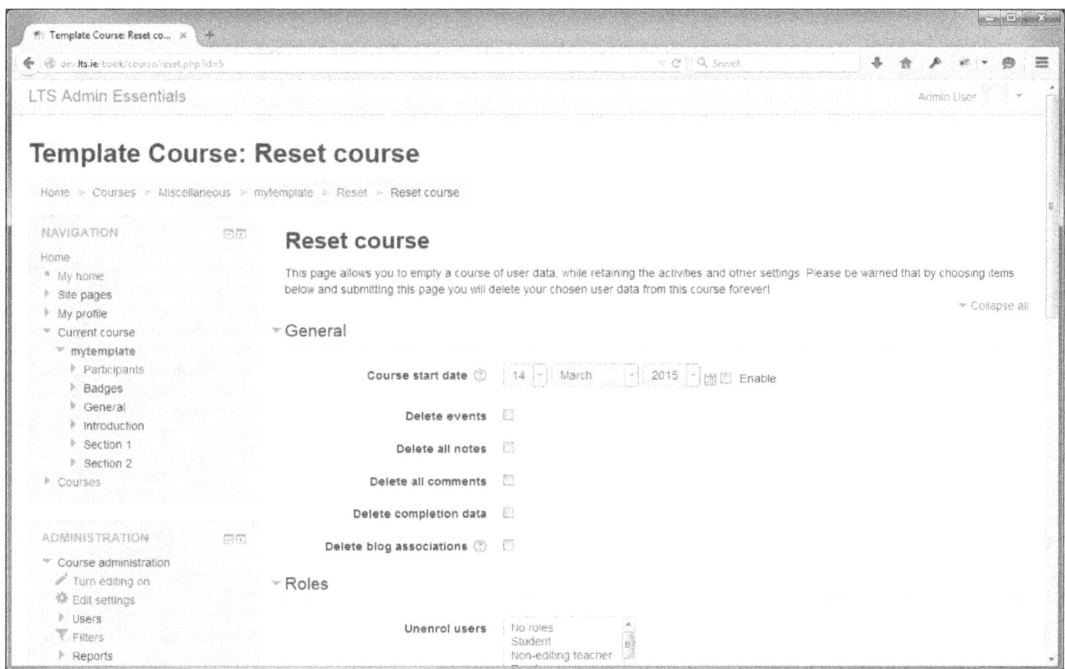

5. Check that everything is as required, then click on the **Reset course** button.
6. A list of updated components will display. Once the reset is completed, click on the **Continue** button.

The course is now reset in Moodle.

Summary

In this chapter, we looked at the administrator's role and the roles of the teachers, when a year-end rollover of a course or courses must be performed. Involving all the stake holders, administrators, student registry, and teaching staff is essential in selecting the right approach.

In the next chapter, we focus on some further administrative tasks on the Moodle site, including monitoring Moodle usage, performance testing, security, and resilience and general settings.

8
Miscellaneous Admin Tasks

In the previous chapter, we looked at the core administrator tasks for end-of-year course rollover management, and the different aspects to consider when deciding which approach to take.

In this chapter, we deal with the remaining admin tasks not covered in the preceding chapters, and at a more advanced level, that many administrators will have to deal with:

- Monitoring Moodle usage
- Performance testing
- Security and resilience
- General settings

Monitoring Moodle usage

There are a number of ways to monitor the usage of the Moodle site. Moodle has a comprehensive logging system, which provides a great audit capability through the provision of a suite of standardized reports. In addition to the logging and reports, Moodle also presents some basic statistics on general usage that can help an administrator understand how the site is being used.

Statistics

Statistics need to be enabled for the site by an administrator, and preferably should be configured to run at quiet times, say, very early morning.

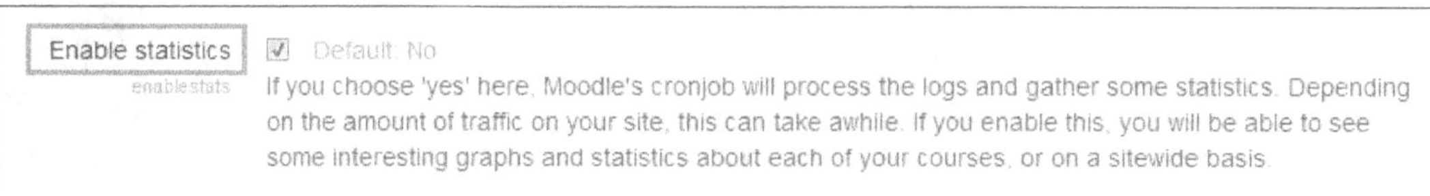

Statistics can also be run manually by an administrator, but note that this will take a while to process completely.

Once they have been compiled, they can then be viewed by navigating to **Administration** | **Site administration** | **Reports** | **Statistics**.

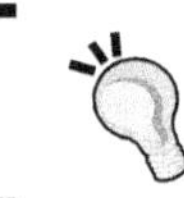

Note that we recommend that you schedule your statistics processing to finish by the time your regular course backup processing is due to begin.

Reports

Moodle has a wide selection of standardized reports available to the administrator to view details on the usage, changes, and performance of the Moodle site. The following reports can all be viewed by navigating to **Administration** | **Site administration** | **Reports** and clicking on the relevant link.

Comments

The **Comments** report generates a list of all comments created on the site by all users:

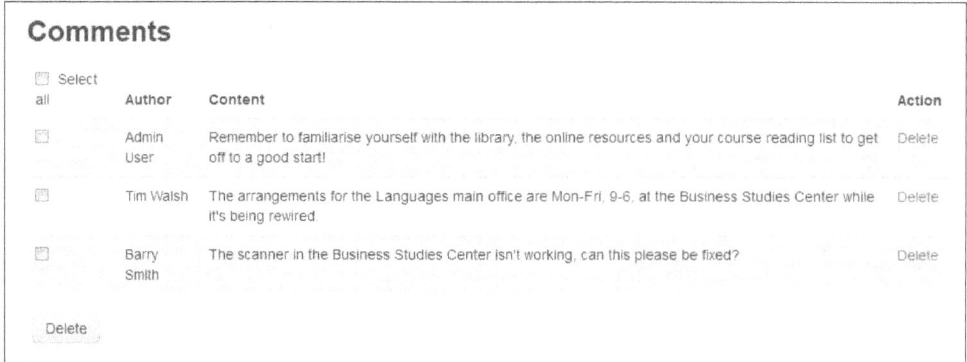

Backups

The **Backups** report generates a list of all recent course backups in descending time and date order. It also indicates when the next scheduled backups are due.

Last execution log

Course	Time taken			Status	Next backup
LTS Moodle Administration Essentials	18 May, 14:37	-	18 May, 14:37	OK	25 May, 11:45
Induction	18 May, 14:37	-	18 May, 14:37	OK	25 May, 11:45
Library Resources	18 May, 14:37	-	18 May, 14:37	OK	25 May, 11:45
Template Course	18 May, 14:37	-	18 May, 14:37	OK	25 May, 11:45

Config changes

The **Config changes** report generates a list of all changes made to any configuration settings by an administrator. It lists the administrator who made the change, and also the old and new value for each setting as relevant:

Config changes

Page: 1 2 3 4 5 6 7 8 9 10 11 12 13 14 15 16 17 18 ...32 (Next)

Date	First name / Surname	Plugin	Setting	New value	Original value
Wednesday, 20 May 2015, 9:20 AM	Admin User	core	statsruntimestartminute	20	5
Wednesday, 20 May 2015, 9:03 AM	Admin User	core	statsfirstrun	1209600	604800
Wednesday, 20 May 2015, 9:03 AM	Admin User	core	statsruntimestartminute	5	0
Wednesday, 20 May 2015, 9:03 AM	Admin User	core	statsruntimestarthour	9	10
Wednesday, 20 May 2015, 8:47 AM	Admin User	core	statsruntimestartminute	0	45

Course overview

The **Course overview** report generates a graph of statistical site usage across courses.

Events list

The **Events list** report generates a list of all events detected on the Moodle site. The list can be further filtered to view more specific information.

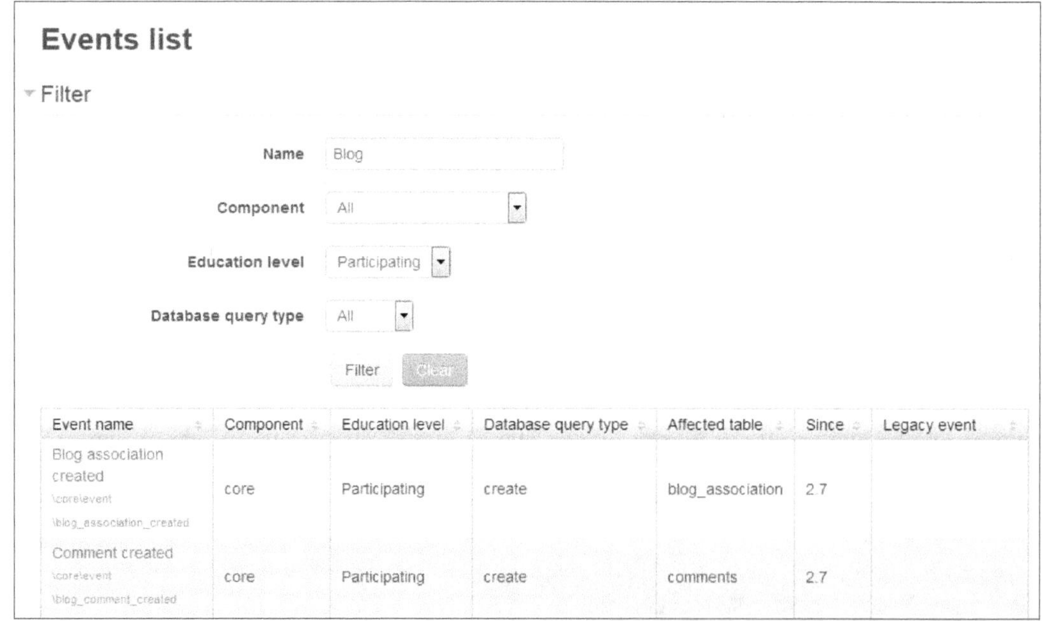

Logs

The **Logs** report generates a list of all logged events detected on the Moodle site. The list can be further filtered to view more specific information.

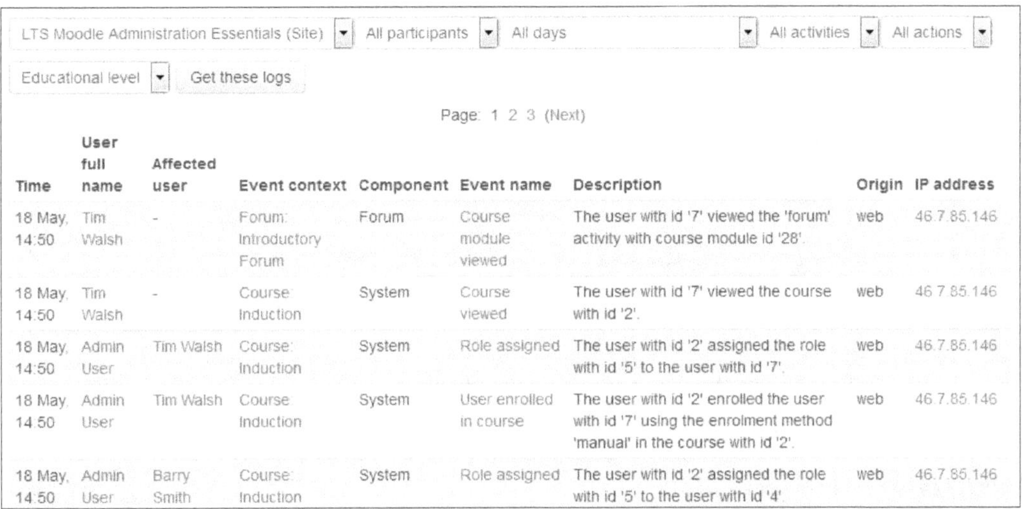
LTS Moodle Administration Essentials (Site) | All participants | All days | All activities | All actions

Educational level | Get these logs

Page: 1 2 3 (Next)

Time	User full name	Affected user	Event context	Component	Event name	Description	Origin	IP address
18 May, 14:50	Tim Walsh	-	Forum: Introductory Forum	Forum	Course module viewed	The user with id '7' viewed the 'forum' activity with course module id '28'.	web	46.7.85.146
18 May, 14:50	Tim Walsh	-	Course: Induction	System	Course viewed	The user with id '7' viewed the course with id '2'.	web	46.7.85.146
18 May, 14:50	Admin User	Tim Walsh	Course: Induction	System	Role assigned	The user with id '2' assigned the role with id '5' to the user with id '7'.	web	46.7.85.146
18 May, 14:50	Admin User	Tim Walsh	Course: Induction	System	User enrolled in course	The user with id '2' enrolled the user with id '7' using the enrolment method 'manual' in the course with id '2'.	web	46.7.85.146
18 May, 14:50	Admin User	Barry Smith	Course: Induction	System	Role assigned	The user with id '2' assigned the role with id '5' to the user with id '4'.	web	46.7.85.146

Live logs

The **Live logs** report generates a list of recent and continuing logged events detected on the Moodle site. This reports every 60 seconds on log events, within the last hour. This list automatically updates when new logged events are detected, unless the **Pause live updates** button has been clicked on.

Pause live updates

Course	Time	User full name	Affected user	Event context	Component	Event name	Description	Origin	IP address
-	18 May, 15:36	Admin User	-	System	Live logs	Live log report viewed	The user with id '2' viewed the live log report for the course with id '0'.	web	46.7.85.146
LTS Admin Essentials	18 May, 15:33	Admin User	-	Front page	Logs	Log report viewed	The user with id '2' viewed the log report for the course with id '1'.	web	46.7.85.146
Induction	18 May, 14:50	Tim Walsh	-	Forum: Introductory Forum	Forum	Course module viewed	The user with id '7' viewed the 'forum' activity with course module id '28'.	web	46.7.85.146
Induction	18 May, 14:50	Tim Walsh	-	Course: Induction	System	Course viewed	The user with id '7' viewed the course with id '2'.	web	46.7.85.146

Performance overview

The **Performance overview** report generates a list of issues, which may affect the performance of the Moodle site and their current status.

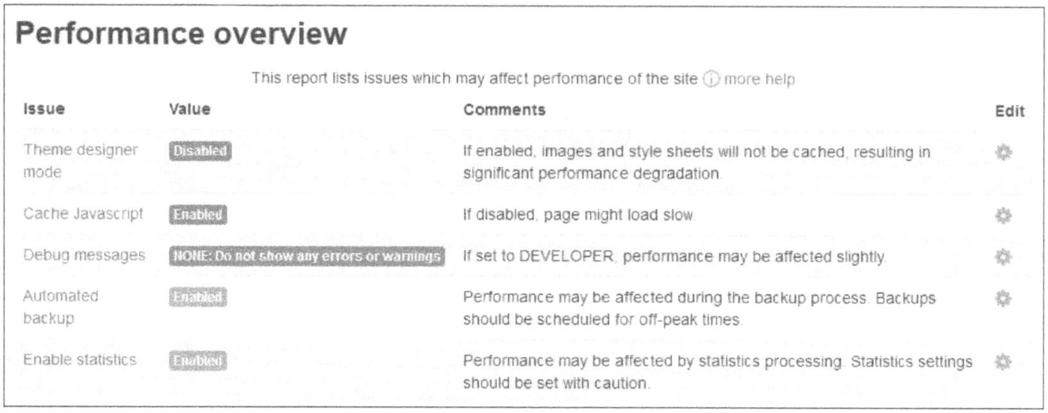

Performance overview

This report lists issues which may affect performance of the site more help

Issue	Value	Comments	Edit
Theme designer mode	Disabled	If enabled, images and style sheets will not be cached, resulting in significant performance degradation	
Cache Javascript	Enabled	If disabled, page might load slow	
Debug messages	NONE: Do not show any errors or warnings	If set to DEVELOPER, performance may be affected slightly	
Automated backup	Enabled	Performance may be affected during the backup process. Backups should be scheduled for off-peak times	
Enable statistics	Enabled	Performance may be affected by statistics processing. Statistics settings should be set with caution.	

Question instances

The **Question instances** report generates a list of all available questions, their contexts within the site, and their question types.

Security overview

The **Security overview** report generates a list of issues, which may affect the security of the Moodle site and their current status.

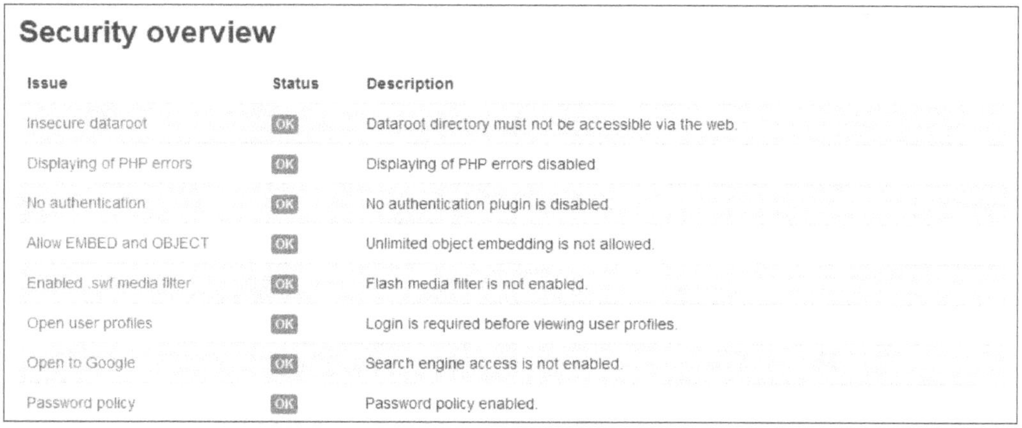

Security overview

Issue	Status	Description
Insecure dataroot	OK	Dataroot directory must not be accessible via the web.
Displaying of PHP errors	OK	Displaying of PHP errors disabled
No authentication	OK	No authentication plugin is disabled
Allow EMBED and OBJECT	OK	Unlimited object embedding is not allowed.
Enabled .swf media filter	OK	Flash media filter is not enabled.
Open user profiles	OK	Login is required before viewing user profiles.
Open to Google	OK	Search engine access is not enabled.
Password policy	OK	Password policy enabled.

Statistics

The **Statistics** report generates a graph of statistical site usage per course.

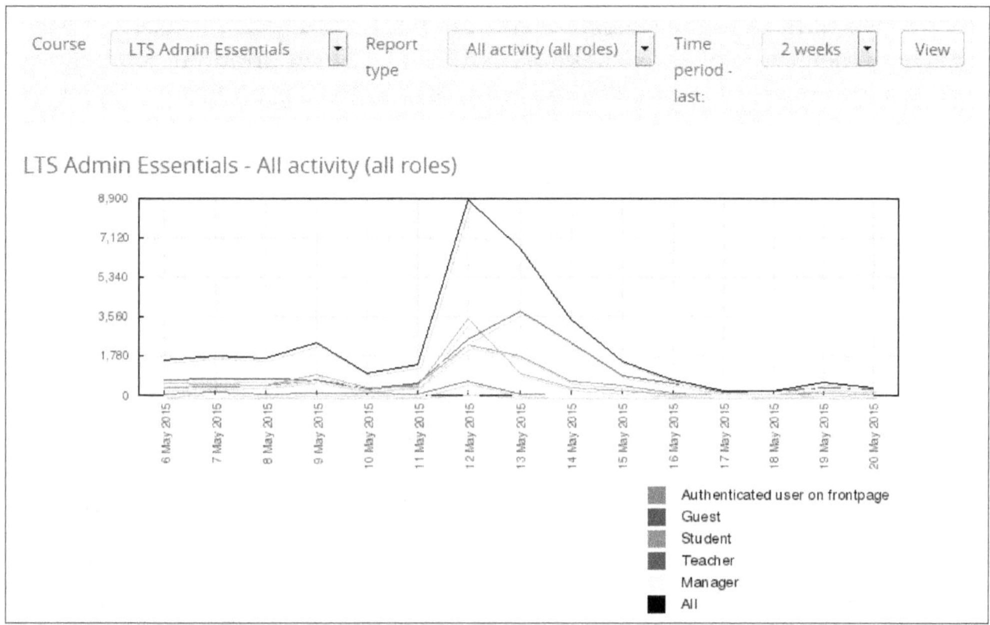

Event monitoring rules

Event monitoring needs to be enabled by an administrator.

You also need to subscribe to monitor event rules, which are created on the **Event monitoring** page under **My profile settings**.

Spam cleaner

The **Spam cleaner** report generates a list of users whose profiles contain searched for strings, which usually indicate that they may be spammer accounts. In this report, we will get two buttons in the operation column per each registered user. These user accounts may then be deleted by clicking on the **Delete user** option if you believe them to be a spammer, or ignored from the report by clicking on **Ignore** if you are sure they are not spam accounts.

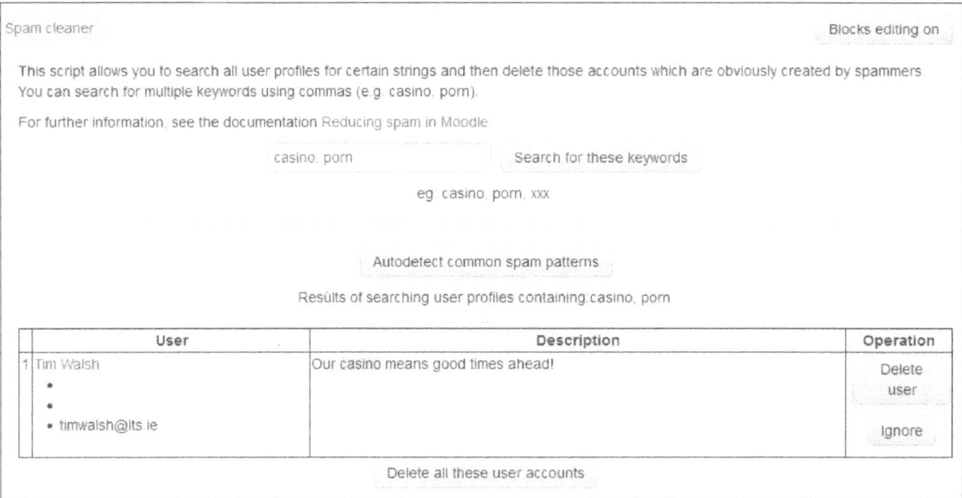

Performance testing

Performance testing helps the administrator understand what the current server setup and configuration can deliver in response times and concurrent users. Moodle has a built-in feature to help generate a **JMeter** script to run and create comparisons between different setups and configurations.

JMeter

Moodle includes a JMeter test plan generator, which is documented at `https://docs.moodle.org/en/JMeter_test_plan_generator`.

JMeter is used to test the performance of websites and other web systems, such as web services. It is built in Java, but can be used to test applications written in any language as it is primarily used to mimic the user using the user interface (web pages and forms) to complete a task.

This tool is for use when testing your site before it is in production and is not recommended for use on a live site. (See: `https://docs.moodle.org/en/JMeter_test_plan_generator`)

JMeter can be used to simulate many users logging in and using the Moodle site at once to test the performance of the infrastructure that hosts the Moodle site.

It uses a script that is created with the steps that the simulated user will follow such as:

- log in
- go to a specific page /course
- view the forum
- view a forum post
- reply to the post
- view the reply
- logout

So using such a script, you can run different numbers of users against your Moodle site to find the stress point, that is, the point at which the server stops performing to your expectations, such as fast response times for loading a course page.

Each time you get JMeter to run the script, you are doing a performance test. By performing repeated tests and making different optimizations to the setup, such as database configuration, it is possible to use JMeter to help you optimize the performance of your existing architecture.

The Moodle JMeter test plan generator is located in the **Administration** block under **Development**. Click on **Make JMeter test plan**.

It can also be accessed via CLI at `admin/tool/generator/cli/maketestplan.php`.

CLI is the Moodle Command Line Interface, where some of the admin features are available to run both through the web interface and via command line.

Note that your Debug messages must be set to **DEVELOPER** in order for JMeter to be enabled, by navigating to **Administration** | **Development** | **Debugging**. Also, you need to configure a test password in your `config.php` script, as follows:

```
// Requirement for JMeter test plan.
$CFG->tool_generator_users_password = "moodle";"
```

Make JMeter test plan

This tool creates a JMeter test plan file along with the user credentials file.

This test plan is designed to work along with https://github.com/moodlehq/moodle-performance-comparison, which makes easier to run the test plan in a specific Moodle environment, gathers information about the runs and compares the results, so you will need to download it and use it's test_runner.sh script or follow the installation and usage instructions.

You need to set a password for the course users in config.php (e.g. $CFG->tool_generator_users_password = 'moodle';). There is no default value for this password to prevent unintended usages of the tool. You need to use the update passwords option in case your course users have other passwords or they were generated by tool_generator but without setting a $CFG->tool_generator_users_password value.

It is part of tool_generator so it works well with the courses generated by the courses and the site generators, it can also be used with any course that contains, at least:

- Enough enrolled users (depends on the test plan size you select) with the password reset to 'moodle'
- A page module instance
- A forum module instance with at least one discussion and one reply

You might want to consider your servers capacity when running large test plans as the amount to load generated by JMeter can be specially big. The ramp up period has been adjusted according to the number of threads (users) to reduce this kind of issues but the load is still huge.

Do not run the test plan on a live system. This feature only creates the files to feed JMeter so is not dangerous by itself, but you should **NEVER** run this test plan in a production site.

Size of course L (1000 users, 6 loops and 100 rampup period)

Test target course Template Course(mytemplate)

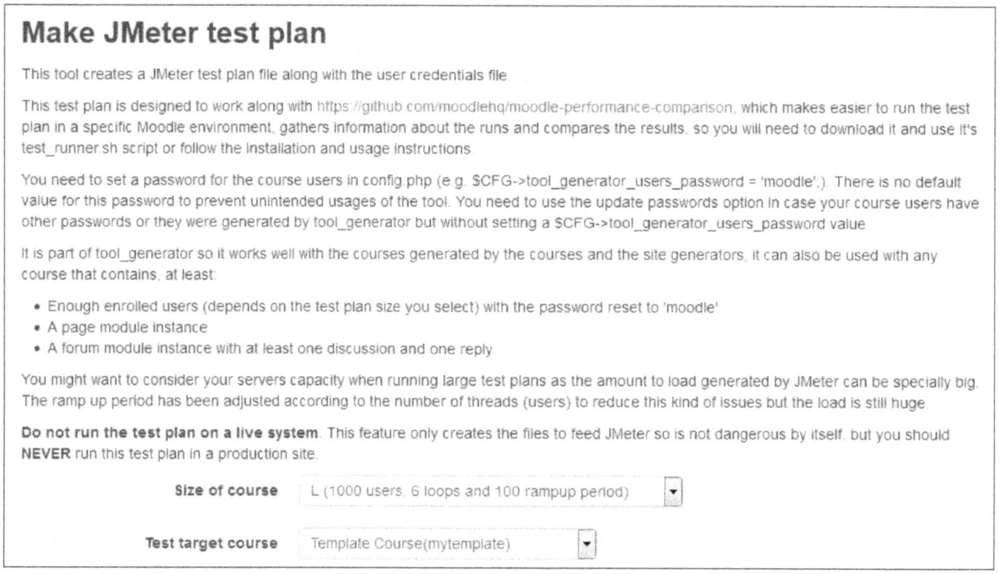

Once this has processed successfully, you will have two links, **Download test plan** and **Download users file** to work with.

Performance comparison

Moodle includes a performance comparison tool, which is documented at `https://github.com/moodlehq/moodle-performance-comparison/blob/master/README.md`.

The Moodle performance comparison tool can help compare:

- Performance before/after applying a patch
- Two different branches performance
- Different configurations and cache stores configurations
- Different hardware
- Web, database, and other services tuning

The Moodle performance comparison can be used to run JMeter test plans and analyze their results.

The Moodle performance comparison is available for download or Git retrieval at `https://github.com/moodlehq/moodle-performance-comparison`.

Once installed in a web server accessible location, the two config scripts need to be copied or renamed and then edited to have your own Moodle settings:

- webserver_config.properties.dist to webserver_config.properties
- jmeter_config.properties.dist to jmeter_config.properties

Security and resilience

These are some general things that you should consider:

- Create regular backups and check whether they are fully restorable
- Run regular updates, both for Moodle and server OS code
- Enable firewalls
- Review open ports
- Force secure passwords
- Check file permissions

Security

Your Moodle site security settings are available by navigating to **Administration** | **Site administration** | **Security**.

IP Blocker

The **IP Blocker page** allows you to configure an **Allowed IP list**, a **Blocked IP list**, and tells you which list to process first. This is useful if you want to limit your Moodle site access to block access from IPs, which are sending you disruptive traffic.

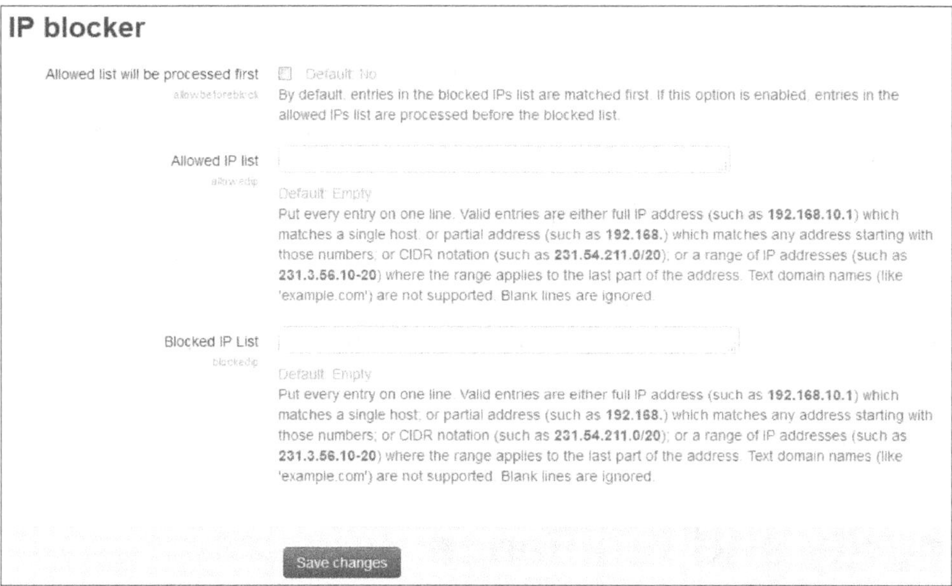

Site policies

The **Site policies** page allows you to configure a great many security settings, including but not limited to forcing log in, user file space limits, allowing **EMBED** or **OBJECT** tags, specifying username characters, **Acceptable Usage Policy** (**AUP**) settings, cron settings, account lockout settings, and specifying required password characters.

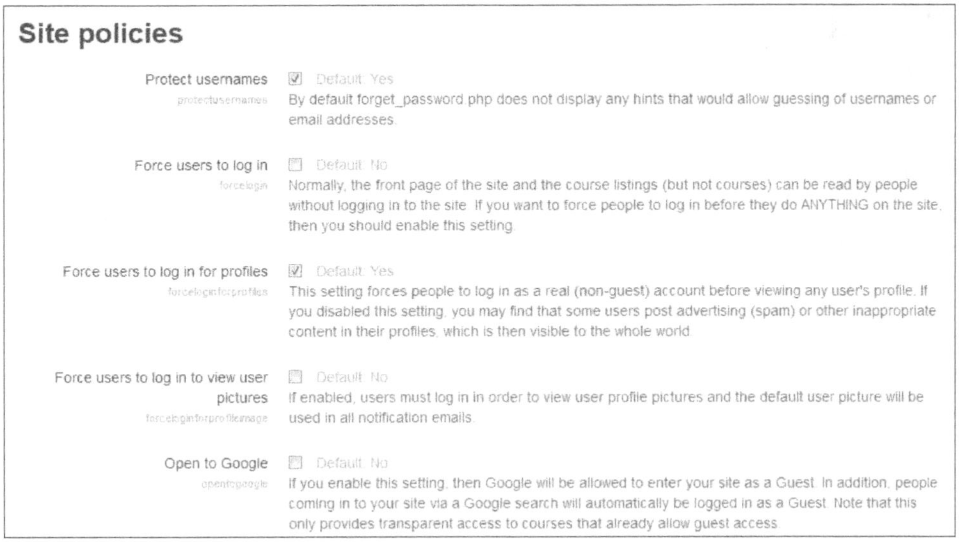

Site policies

Protect usernames
protectusernames
☑ Default: Yes
By default forget_password.php does not display any hints that would allow guessing of usernames or email addresses.

Force users to log in
forcelogin
☐ Default: No
Normally, the front page of the site and the course listings (but not courses) can be read by people without logging in to the site. If you want to force people to log in before they do ANYTHING on the site, then you should enable this setting.

Force users to log in for profiles
forceloginforprofiles
☑ Default: Yes
This setting forces people to log in as a real (non-guest) account before viewing any user's profile. If you disabled this setting, you may find that some users post advertising (spam) or other inappropriate content in their profiles, which is then visible to the whole world.

Force users to log in to view user pictures
forceloginforprofileimage
☐ Default: No
If enabled, users must log in in order to view user profile pictures and the default user picture will be used in all notification emails.

Open to Google
opentogoogle
☐ Default: No
If you enable this setting, then Google will be allowed to enter your site as a Guest. In addition, people coming in to your site via a Google search will automatically be logged in as a Guest. Note that this only provides transparent access to courses that already allow guest access.

HTTP security

The **HTTP security** page allows you to configure a number of settings related to HTTP, such as enforcing HTTPS for the login page only, cookie management, and preventing password autocompletion.

HTTP security

Use HTTPS for logins
loginhttps
☐ Default: No
Turning this on will make Moodle use a secure https connection just for the login page (providing a secure login), and then afterwards revert back to the normal http URL for general speed. CAUTION: this setting REQUIRES https to be specifically enabled on the web server - if it is not then YOU COULD LOCK YOURSELF OUT OF YOUR SITE.

Secure cookies only
cookiesecure
☐ Default: No
If server is accepting only https connections it is recommended to enable sending of secure cookies. If enabled please make sure that web server is not accepting http:// or set up permanent redirection to https:// address. When *wwwroot* address does not start with https:// this setting is turned off automatically.

Only http cookies
cookiehttponly
☐ Default: No
Enables new PHP 5.2.0 feature - browsers are instructed to send cookie with real http requests only, cookies should not be accessible by scripting languages. This is not supported in all browsers and it may not be fully compatible with current code. It helps to prevent some types of XSS attacks.

Allow frame embedding
allowframembedding
☐ Default: No
Allow embedding of this site in frames on external sites. Enabling of this feature is not recommended for security reasons.

Prevent password autocompletion on login form
loginpasswordautocomplete
☐ Default: No
If enabled, users are not allowed to save their account password in their browser.

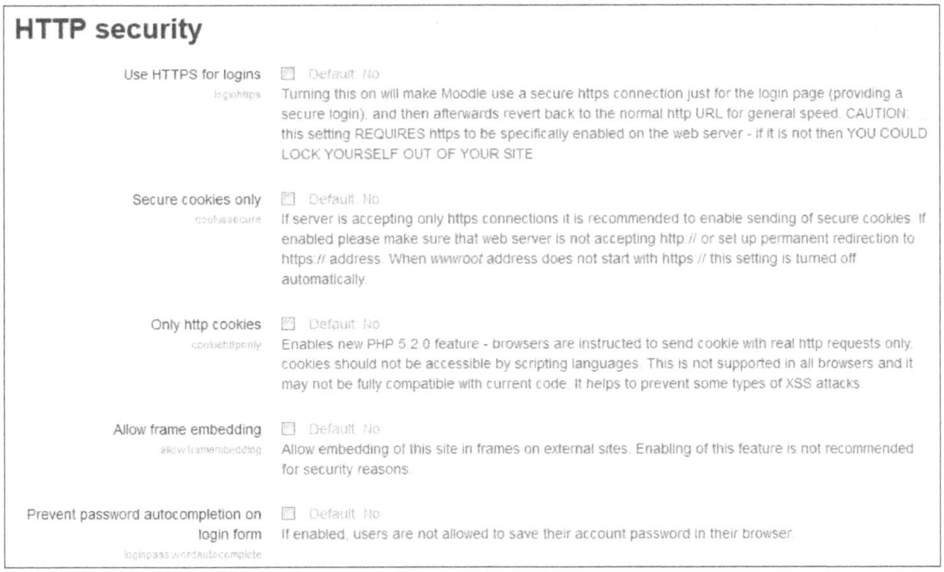

Notifications

The **Notifications** page allows you to configure e-mail notifications in the event of login failures over a set threshold.

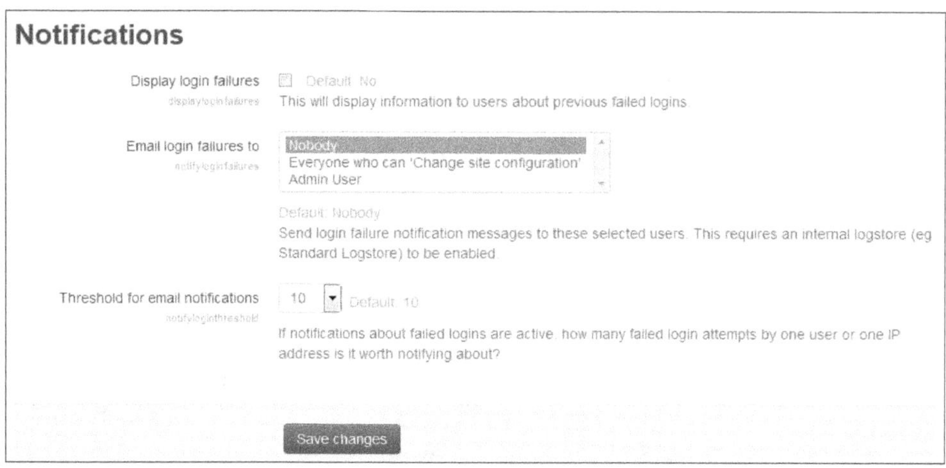

Anti-Virus

The **Anti-Virus** page allows you to configure **clam AV**, an open source (GPL) anti-virus engine, available at `http://www.clamav.net/index.html`, to securely process e-mail scanning, web scanning, and file scanning.

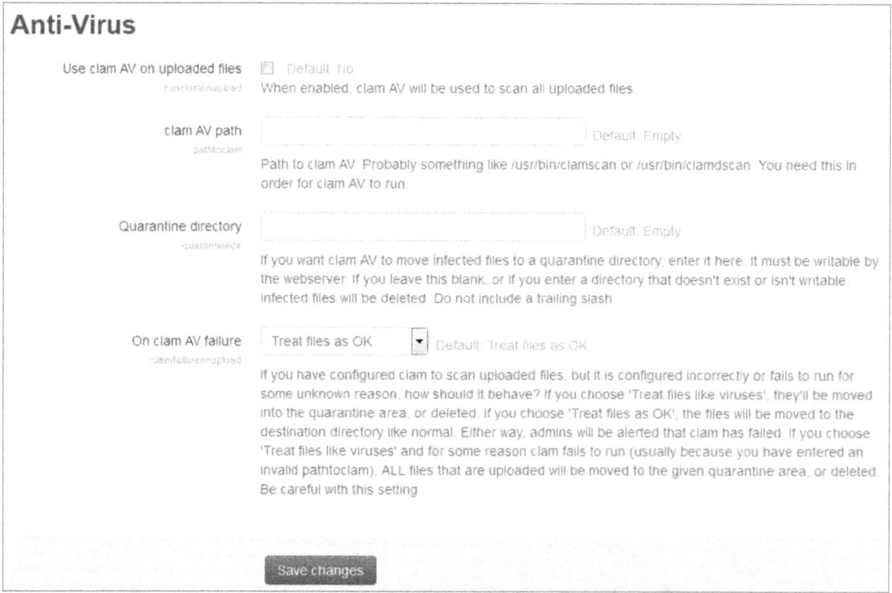

Security overview report

An overview report is available by navigating to **Administration** | **Site administration** | **Reports** | **Security overview**.

This report provides a quick audit of a number of settings on the site with a **Status** field letting you know if they are **OK** and require no checking, or if they warrant a **Warning** and should be checked, or if they are serious and require attention, it reports them as **Critical**.

General considerations

These are some other general things that you should consider in managing your Moodle site:

Force users to log in

Guard your Moodle site content and IP—consider forcing users to log in.

This prevents any anonymous viewer from seeing your default front page without logging in beforehand.

This page can potentially display sensitive information, such as course names and summaries, news items, or even calendar events.

Equally, however, you need to consider if your front page is being used as marketing, and therefore do not want to lock anonymous users out.

Navigate to **Administration** | **Site administration** | **Security** | **Site policies** and check on **Force users to log in**.

You can also force users to login for profiles, which will protect your users privacy by forcing a user to be logged in before they can view another users profile.

Disable log in as a guest

This prevents any anonymous viewer from logging in with guest access and with no need for a valid login. Once the **Guest Login** button is hidden, only authenticated users will be permitted access preventing anonymous users from logging into the site.

Navigate to **Administration** | **Site administration** | **Advanced features** and select `Hide` for the **Guest login** button.

Enable timezones

If your server has not been configured with a `php.ini` timezone setting, then this should be configured on your Moodle site to deal with many timezone customizations, particularly daylight saving time or summer time, which affects many of us.

Navigate to **Administration** | **Site administration** | **Location** | **Update timezone** and upload the supported timezones from the supplied link URLs.

Then, navigate to **Administration** | **Site administration** | **Location** | **Location settings**, set your relevant **Default timezone**, and click on **Save changes**.

By default, users can also set their own timezone in their profile settings.

Enable cron

Cron is required for many essential Moodle site features, including messages, e-mails, activity completions, and other background processing.

Enabling cron depends on your host server OS and configuration. You may need to ask your hosting support for documentation.

On UNIX-based systems, for instance, logged in as root, type the following:

```
$ crontab -u www-data -e
```

In the editor window, add the following line:

```
*/5 * * * * /usr/bin/php  /path/to/moodle/admin/cli/cron.php >/dev/null
```

This will run the site cron every 5 minutes, and discard the resulting logging data.

Debug messages

This displays essential detailed error warnings to help investigate problems, such as blank screens, data loss, or values not being saved correctly. This can typically happen after manual code changes, or installing new plugins or development work.

Navigate to **Administration** | **Site administration** | **Development** | **Debugging**, select `DEVELOPER` for **Debug messages**, and click on **Save changes**.

Then tick **Display debug messages** so that the error messages will show.

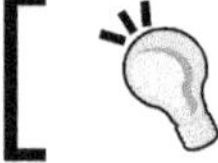

Remember to change **Debug messages** back to `NORMAL` or `NONE` when you're done.

Purge all caches

Purging your Moodle site cache is safe to do anytime, and keeps the site up-to-date, but the downside is the site will be initially slower as the cache rebuilds. If you have made any theme code or JavaScript changes, this is an essential step.

Navigate to **Administration** | **Site administration** | **Development** | **Purge all caches** and click on **Purge all caches**.

Enhancing the My Home page or Dashboard

You can add extra core Moodle blocks to the default **My Home page** or **Dashboard** as it's known as in 2.9 onwards, or you can add third party-plugins, which generate specific information, such as timelines, reports, or event alerts.

Navigate to **Administration** | **Site administration** | **Appearance** | **Default My home page** where you can add and remove blocks as required.

Users are allowed to customize their **My Home page**, but this can be disabled if needed, for instance, if your institution has a preset static collection of **My Home** blocks to show.

Navigate to **Administration** | **Site administration** | **Users** | **Permissions** | **Define roles**, search for and untick the `moodle/my:manageblocks` capability in the **Authenticated User** role page, and click on **Save changes**.

Language customization

Your institution may have a localized terminology or phrases, which you may prefer to use over standard Moodle phrases.

Every single piece of text displayed in Moodle is customizable.

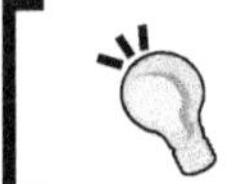

Note that this is different to course role renaming, where you can switch students to participants, teachers to facilitators, and so on.

Navigate to **Administration** | **Site administration** | **Language** | **Language customization** and click the **Open Language pack for editing** option. Select the relevant options in the forms until you get to **Filter strings** page.

Shift-select all the script values for **Show strings of these components**. Type in the string to filter on in **Only strings containing**. Click on **Show strings**.

Make the **Local customization** text changes as required, save the changes, and remember to run **Purge all Caches** to update the string caches.

Enabling site administrators

You may need to allow a colleague or other person administrator level access to your Moodle site, either permanently or temporarily.

Instead of giving them the site administrator users' credentials, you can promote their existing account to that of a site administrator.

Navigate to **Administration** | **Site administration** | **Users** | **Permissions** | **Site administrators** where you can add and remove users as required.

This maintains the security of your Moodle site, and your master admin login as site administrators can be removed at any time, once their admin level access is no longer needed.

Note that giving someone administrator access gives them control over the whole site and access to all of the courses, accounts, and student data, so be careful in doing this.

Enabling maintenance mode

You can enable maintenance mode when needed to prevent non-admin users from accessing the site while you perform updates, backups, or plugin installations, and then disable it when done.

Navigate to **Administration** | **Site administration** | **Server** | **Maintenance mode** where you can enable and disable maintenance mode as required.

You can also add a message to be displayed to all users, such as letting users know at what time the site will be available again.

Support contact details

You can provide specific support contact details to use, to avoid the Moodle site using the master admin name and e-mail.

This is especially important if it's your own e-mail, and you are not responsible for handling general student support.

Navigate to **Administration** | **Site administration** | **Server** | **Support contact** to specify a support name, e-mail, and even a page URL.

Administration search box

The **Administration** search box is normally located at the bottom of the **Administration** block with a **Go** button to start the search.

Whatever phrase, activity, or setting you're looking for, it will display the matching results as found. Hence, it is incredibly useful for searching for anything!

The results page even allows you to alter some settings, if they are tick boxes or dropdowns, and save them with one click on the **Save changes** button.

Summary

In this chapter, we looked at a number of additional administrator tasks not covered in the preceding chapters. Although these will not always be relevant, having an understanding of these extra options will help you should a related issue arise.

In this book, we looked at the core tasks typically undertaken by every Moodle administrator in some way or another.

Whether you install Moodle on your own server, or get a hosting contract from a Moodle Service Provider, understanding what is involved will help you in the implementation.

User management is one of the things that you will need to decide once, but it is fundamental to your ongoing site maintenance. Give sufficient planning to decide how you will add users to the site and how you will authenticate users now and in the future. Remember that you can always make a change later on if needed.

The site structure is key to the whole user experience for course creators, teachers, and students, so getting this structure correct before you add users to courses is key. It can be a long task making substantial changes to the structure and the default course template layout later on, when you have hundreds of courses set up. This can lead to confusion among users.

More and more organizations centrally manage the adding of teachers and students to their courses; however, having a good understanding of what roles are, and how they can be altered, will save you time later on. It is normal to have multiple enrolment methods enabled—so as with user management, changes can happen later.

Moodle has many features for both teaching and learning; however, with a lot of excellent enhancements available as plugins (including integrations with systems Office 365), you should look at what extra features you want to add to the site. Just be careful and sure to test sufficiently before adding them to a production or live site.

Most institutions will perform some type of end of course rollover process. It is always going to be different for different institutions, due to their scheduling and methodology of teaching. Find the right process for your organization that has the least downtime and that is most practical.

Lastly, this book tackled some additional administrative options that you can implement. This book is not meant to be everything an administrator can do, but instead is just focused on the core tasks that you need to understand to get your Moodle site live and running.

The Moodle community is very helpful, so if you run into any problems, be sure to check out the `https://moodle.org/` forums for help, or consider getting paid-for support from a certified Moodle provider from `https://moodle.com/`.

Index

N

P

Q

R

S

U

Thank you for buying
Moodle Administration Essentials

About Packt Publishing

Packt, pronounced 'packed', published its first book, *Mastering phpMyAdmin for Effective MySQL Management*, in April 2004, and subsequently continued to specialize in publishing highly focused books on specific technologies and solutions.

Our books and publications share the experiences of your fellow IT professionals in adapting and customizing today's systems, applications, and frameworks. Our solution-based books give you the knowledge and power to customize the software and technologies you're using to get the job done. Packt books are more specific and less general than the IT books you have seen in the past. Our unique business model allows us to bring you more focused information, giving you more of what you need to know, and less of what you don't.

Packt is a modern yet unique publishing company that focuses on producing quality, cutting-edge books for communities of developers, administrators, and newbies alike. For more information, please visit our website at `www.packtpub.com`.

About Packt Open Source

In 2010, Packt launched two new brands, Packt Open Source and Packt Enterprise, in order to continue its focus on specialization. This book is part of the Packt Open Source brand, home to books published on software built around open source licenses, and offering information to anybody from advanced developers to budding web designers. The Open Source brand also runs Packt's Open Source Royalty Scheme, by which Packt gives a royalty to each open source project about whose software a book is sold.

Writing for Packt

We welcome all inquiries from people who are interested in authoring. Book proposals should be sent to `author@packtpub.com`. If your book idea is still at an early stage and you would like to discuss it first before writing a formal book proposal, then please contact us; one of our commissioning editors will get in touch with you.

We're not just looking for published authors; if you have strong technical skills but no writing experience, our experienced editors can help you develop a writing career, or simply get some additional reward for your expertise.

[PACKT] open source
community experience distilled
PUBLISHING

Moodle 2 Administration

ISBN: 978-1-84951-604-4 Paperback: 420 pages

An administrator's guide to configuring, securing, customizing, and extending Moodle

1. A complete guide for planning, installing, optimizing, customizing, and configuring Moodle.
2. Learn how to network and extend Moodle for your needs and integrate with other systems.
3. A complete reference of all Moodle system settings.

Moodle 2.0 E-Learning Course Development

ISBN: 978-1-84951-526-9 Paperback: 344 pages

A complete guide to successful learning using Moodle

1. The new book and ebook edition of the best selling introduction to using Moodle for teaching and e-learning, updated for Moodle 2.0.
2. Straightforward coverage of installing and using the Moodle system, suitable for newcomers as well as existing Moodle users who want to get a few tips.
3. A unique course-based approach focuses your attention on designing well-structured, interactive, and successful courses.

Please check **www.PacktPub.com** for information on our titles

www.ingramcontent.com/pod-product-compliance
Lightning Source LLC
LaVergne TN
LVHW061223100826
845148LV00004B/840
9781784395476